The Netherlands Architecture Institute

The Netherlands Architecture Institute

Texts
Ruud Brouwers
Jo Coenen
Kristin Feireiss
Mariet Willinge

Photographical essay
Jannes Linders

NAI Publishers

Contents

Policy and building

Kristin Feireiss

This second edition of the book about the Netherlands Architecture Institute (NAI) comes at a memorable moment. In 1998 the NAI celebrates its tenth anniversary and it is five years since Queen Beatrix officially opened Jo Coenen's building on 29 October 1993. The building contains all the elements of the NAI: the collection, the exhibition halls, NAI Publishers and the journal *Archis*.

From its very inception, the institute has functioned as a lively centre of architecture for the professional community and the public at large, a role that will be expanded in the future. The early years, immediately following the move to the new building, were mainly devoted to establishing the new institute. More recently, and especially since my arrival in 1996, the focus has been on opening up the institute to the outside world. In addition to the existing wide range of tasks, new initiatives have been taken aimed at extending national and international collaboration.

This book contains articles dealing specifically with the history of the design commission, the premises and sources of inspiration informing the design, and the scope and role of the collection. In my foreword I would therefore like to concentrate on two other aspects: on the one hand the concept that underpins our work and serves as the guideline in developing our programme, on the other hand the question of how the building and the activities that take place there complement, influence and perhaps even reinforce one another.

Policy

As I see it, sound policy requires a critical analysis of the current situation of architectural museums and institutes, and of their missions and opportunities.

For such an analysis, it is important to realize that museums all over the world are undergoing changes. These range from a re-orientation of function, partly as a result of a change in the make-up of their viewing public, to a revaluation of their very raison d'être in the age of new media, increasing interconnection and ongoing digitization. When we consider the specific function and mission of the architectural museum it is against the background of these general developments.

In my opinion, there is a fundamental difference between an architectural museum and an art museum. Indeed, I would go so far as to say that architecture is not art. Put it another way: the undoubtedly great artistic value of individual works is an extremely pleasing side-effect, but does not in itself justify their display in an architectural museum. The primary justification for inclusion, in my view, is not the artistic aspect but the concept and context of the design. This includes such things as theoretical and historical background, design and building process, strategy seeking, complexity and approach.

Another important distinction is that art objects, paintings, drawings, sculptures and video installations are all end products of the creative act, if I may be so prosaic. Architectural drawings, models, computer animations and photographs are only stages on the way to realization – the end product is usually the completed building.

The question is, therefore: How is content conveyed during this interim stage towards realization? And, much more importantly: Why is it done? What are the responsibilities of architectural museums?

My personal view is founded in the belief that present-day architectural museums have both a social and a cultural mission. An architectural museum performs a useful function:

when it understands that architectural planning and urban development are vital ingredients of social life and cultural policy, and when it provides information on and talks about these interconnections;
when it endeavours to start or stimulate or keep alive an international dialogue on architectural planning and urban development;
when it uses the various means at its disposal (exhibitions, lectures, discussions, symposia, publications) to try to present and to influence current developments in this field;
when it uses its own research to focus on the history of architecture and to place current developments in a historical context;
when it takes seriously its role as mediator and intermediary between professionals and non-professionals, as well as between specialists from different disciplines;
when its new ventures contribute to a qualitative improvement in present-day construction practice;
when it tries to make the general public sympathetic to environmental questions so that the public can better understand, observe and protect its own everyday environment.

This is not meant to sound like the Ten Commandments for Architectural Museums, but I do believe it makes sense to define objectives clearly. Phrases like 'should try to' or 'should concern itself with' merely fudge the issue, creating the impression that the objectives are unlikely to be achieved.

We should be aware of the fact that we – the architectural museums – want something from the public, not the other way round. It is our aim and our challenge to communicate a difficult subject and we need the public's co-operation.

My main interest is to open up the NAI for a wider public and to create a lively forum for the discussion on architecture, city planning and related disciplines. The strategy for achieving this aim consists, in my view, of the following elements which determine the programme: continuity, actuality, an open attitude towards different concepts and international dialogue. We are an institute for architectural research, a laboratory for experiments and a place for events. After two years spent pursuing this policy concept at the NAI, rapidly increasing visitor numbers and growing national and international interest seem to indicate that we are on the right course.

Having touched on why we should communicate architecture, I would now like to focus on the question of whom we want to communicate with. Which public do we want to reach? In my opinion it should be a very diverse one, people of all ages with different levels of education and different interests: children, students, professionals (i.e. architects, architecture historians, engineers, city planners, landscape architects, sociologists, etc) and the general public – the non-professionals.

My strategy with regard to exhibitions is: information, confrontation, provocation, stimulation and entertainment, with different concepts for each different group of visitors.

Two years ago, for example, we set up the SchoolAtelier and Treasure Room especially for school children. The aim of these activities is to make children and young people more aware of the built environment and to make it clear to them in a fun way that architecture is part of our daily lives and that it can have both a negative and a positive effect on the quality of life.

For students and young architects from the Netherlands and abroad we hold yearly (now twice yearly) masterclasses and workshops, each of which attracts participants from more

Exhibition 'Daniel Libeskind, Beyond the Wall', NAI 1997

than ten countries worldwide. We also organize competitions for young architects and designers and we are developing close working relationships with university architecture departments at Delft University of Technology, TU Berlin and Harvard University, among others.

Exhibitions

It is important to remember that architectural exhibitions display only the two-dimensional drawing, not the three-dimensional finished object – the completed building – and that models, computer animations and photographs are no substitutes for reality – the building itself. Indeed, this must never be the aim of an exhibition, as we are not trying to approximate reality. Instead, exhibitions must place architecture in a different context. More complex common elements must be revealed and comparisons made possible – and this must be done in the most imaginative, vivid, impressive and emotive way possible, given the subject. A successful presentation demands that there be both information and enjoyment. But how to create such a dialogue and emotional rapport between people and an architectural object?

It is certainly not enough simply to satisfy the thirst for knowledge, nor is a purely didactic approach the answer. Employing the various media I referred to above is not enough to stop the visitor from being just a detached observer either. Every exhibition must be tailor-made. What is required is a design that gives people an emotional experience and that also gives the visitor room to think and gets them actively involved. This means that a new focus is needed, and that concentration must alternate with relaxation, entertainment with information, and all must go hand in hand with sensory experiences.

The above concept must take into account the professional's need for information as well as the non–professional's need to be entertained (and vice versa). I would like to mention one example of what I would deem a successful exhibition: successful in the sense that it satisfied the above–mentioned criteria and conveyed a feeling for architecture.

The 1997 exhibition 'Daniel Libeskind, Beyond the Wall' was an experiment and a risky one at that. The installation, designed by Daniel Libeskind, was a sculpture in itself, a building within a building consisting of 1800 square metres of steel panels. Visitors were confronted with a labyrinthine installation of nine metre-high leaning walls which had a physical impact on their experience of space and helped them to understand the work of this architect as expressed in over forty models and a hundred drawings.

The general public we want to reach will only develop an awareness of architecture and will only become interested in environmental questions if it is emotionally engaged by what we have to offer.

Collaboration

A brief foreword for a book that is primarily about the NAI building, naturally offers little scope for an inclusive account of the various areas in which we are involved or of the broad spectrum of activities such as exhibitions, lectures, workshops and symposia that we organize. However, the most important thing is, as I have already said, not to see architecture as an isolated entity but as a vital part of social life and cultural policy.

Second International NAI Summer Masterclass with Kees Christiaanse and Matthias Sauerbruch, August 1997

This is why the collaboration with other organizations, academic disciplines and artistic specialties is a vital part of our work. The museum must literally step outside and get involved with social and cultural life. This entails, among other things, organizing competitions (sometimes together with other organizations); taking an active part in the annual Rotterdam Film Festival with exhibitions about film architecture; initiating multicultural events like South African Seasons which prompted a response from nearly all Rotterdam's cultural institutions; devising and organizing international symposia on topical and contro-versial themes like the conference 'Museum of the future, the future of the museum', the international symposium 'Inventing the Future', held to celebrate the tenth anniversary of the NAI, conferences on international airport design and the Any conference which in 1997 was held in the NAI. All these initiatives and activities exemplify the NAI's role as forum for the national and international dialogue about architecture and urbanism.

The Building

For me, this museum building by Jo Coenen has been a challenge from the very beginning. In fact it all started when, on my first visit as newly appointed director, I was unable to find the entrance. From that moment onward I was totally engrossed by the building and that is unlikely to change much in the coming years. That the design is a masterly feat of urbanism on a difficult site is beyond dispute in my opinion, as is the high architectural and conceptual quality of the design. But how to engage with the building? How to play on it? How to bring it to life?

My first impression was that it was a virtual fortress, enclosed on two sides by water. Even though the building is partially glazed, you first have to cross a bridge or climb a flight of steps and pass through a long arcade to get to it. Only then does the huge entrance lobby open up, though it contains nothing to suggest that this is an architectural museum. It might just as well be the elegant entrance of some corporate headquarters. Once inside you cross a second bridge and still you have no idea where the exhibition halls are located. Finally, via a platform and a lift to the basement, you reach the main exhibition space: some 1000 square metres floor area, nine metres high and with a 30 metre-long glass wall overlooking the water. It evokes an overwhelming spatial sensation and the spontaneous reaction: what a pity this space cannot always remain empty. For those who called upon to orchestrate the space, a second question immediately presents itself: how to arrange an exhibition here that not only fulfils the conditions of the exhibition programme but also does full justice to the space.

This building, in all its subtle layering, with all its quirks and with its singularity, has continued to engross me – a process that is by no means over – in much the same way as a human being will sometimes do. Someone you are fascinated by but do not quite know how to deal with. With a mixture of curiosity, fascination and respect, I started to bring my own impression of

NAI-bookshop seen from the bridge leading to the entrance

the building into harmony with the existing situation and I have noted with surprise that the building responds and adapts without losing its individual character. Each time that I have changed something, it has looked as if it was always meant to be that way. The entrance lobby has become an interesting exhibition space with many design possibilities, yet the transparent character of the space has remained intact. The billboards on the facades with information about the various exhibitions and other attractions (archives, library, SchoolAtelier, bookshop and café) do not disturb the overall appearance and have an inviting quality.

One side of the gallery surrounding the large exhibition hall has been colonized by the SchoolAtelier. Here, on long, metal benches, children and young people from eight to eighteen years of age draw and construct. Above them, the upper hall, which was in fact never intended to be open to the public, was soon pressed into service for exhibitions and several times a year it is used as a workplace for students and young architects. Even the lawn that encloses two sides of the exhibition building is no longer exempt from museum activities. In the summer of 1998 it saw its first exhibition, a display of new garden shed designs. But the process of opening up – as regards both content and design – is by no means finished yet.

Kristin Feireiss has been Director of the Netherlands Architecture Institute since 1996.

The collection, backbone of the NAI

Mariet Willinge

Among the wide variety of activities undertaken by the NAI, the collection occupies a special position. This is already evident from outside of the building, for the collection is housed in the gently curving, almost blank-walled north wing along Rochussenstraat, linked only by a transparent bridge to the other parts of the building. In both structure and content, the collection is the backbone of the institute.

One of the NAI's main tasks as formulated in its founding charter, is 'to bring together, maintain and make accessible, collections, archives, library and documentation relating to Dutch architecture and urban planning'. This, then, is the field of activity of the Collections Department, sometimes as part of the Institute's many and varied activities, often as a constant factor with its own parameters.

This complex of activities also points up the special nature of the NAI: an institute that is more than just a museum. For the NAI is also archive, research institute, library, centre for contemporary (international) architecture, publisher and forum for informed debate.

The collection, unlike most museum collections, is not merely the basis for the NAI's own exhibition policy but also fulfils a much broader function. It is a source and resource for many different kinds of research, for the dissemination and augmentation of knowledge about the history of Dutch architecture and urban planning, for the preservation of historic buildings, for academic study and research and for information about the Dutch built environment.

The combination of architectural archives and a specialized library is an enormous asset for researchers. Archival research is strengthened and supported by the availability of up-to-date literature, while library research into certain facets of architecture acquires added depth by the presence of the relevant archives. Moreover, the presence of so many and such important archives also enables researchers to conduct a broad sweep of the archives.

As such, the collection serves many more uses and users than could be served by exhibitions alone.

A brief history

With the founding of the NAI in 1988, the architectural collections accumulated during the very long preparatory period (over a hundred years), finally acquired a worthy place in the wide range of cultural institutions in the Netherlands.

Although people had been collecting architectural archives and talking and dreaming about an architectural museum for much longer, the basis of the present collection was laid in the 1920s. As to the institute, its basis was laid in the middle of the nineteenth century with the setting up of two organizations that were to play a crucial role in the prehistory of the present institute: the Maatschappij tot Bevordering der Bouwkunst (Society for the Promotion of Architecture, known simply as 'de Maatschappij') in 1842, and the Genootschap Architectura et Amicitia (A et A) in 1856. De Maatschappij was intended not just for the profession but for everybody who was interested in architecture. It actively promoted architecture, among other things by organizing debates on such important issues as the 'style' problem and technical innovations. An account of these discussions could be read in the society's journal, Bouwkundige Bijdragen.

In addition to their regular journals, both de Maatschappij and A et A, an association of practising architects, published illustrated works.[1] Both organizations were quick to recognize and exploit the importance of exhibitions. Competitions were held and the entries displayed at various occasions. These exhibitions stressed the cultural and artistic dimension of architecture, in other words they went beyond the technical-structural side which until then had been regarded as the most important aspect of architecture. The two societies were also active outside the Netherlands. In 1902, for example, they joined forces to present the Dutch entry for the First International Exhibition of Decorative Art, held in Turin.

Since these activities were directed mainly at a professional audience, there was at first little motivation to try to reach a wider public, for example by setting up an architectural museum, although this idea was raised within A et A as early as 1867 by the architect J.H. Leliman.

The archives of de Maatschappij and A et A that have been preserved are now part of the collection of the NAI where they are an important source for research into the NAI's own history.[2]

Although a large part of de Maatschappij's collection of drawings was destroyed by fire in 1916, the two hundred or so drawings that survived give some idea of the richness of this collection.

It was not until 1912 that the idea of arousing interest among a wider audience began to be openly canvassed. In that year the architect J.H.W. Leliman, son of J.H. Leliman, issued a fervent plea for the establishment of an architectural museum[3] in *De Bouwwereld*, a journal he had launched in 1902. Initial reactions were somewhat lukewarm and although A et A responded by setting up a committee to look into the possibility of such a museum, nothing concrete came of it.

Leliman, who wanted architects' design drawings to be accorded the same status as the drawings and sketches of other artists, suggested building up a collection of drawings and models. He even considered the possibility of merging such a collection with other collections, like those held by the Technical College in Delft which had a long-standing collection of books, journals, photographs and casts of architectural fragments.

The A et A committee was later replaced by a national commission to advise the minister of Arts and Sciences about the feasibility of setting up a national architectural museum. There was plenty of discussion about the nature and location of such a museum: should it be linked to the State Academy in Amsterdam or, perhaps a better option, to the architectural faculty at the Technical College in Delft? Should such a museum be aimed exclusively at architecture students, or did they want to reach a wider audience? Should architecture be regarded as art and the architectural museum consequently as an art museum? That they were unable to resolve these questions is evident from the fact that it was not until 1988 that the present architectural institute was established. Nonetheless, many other initiatives were taken over the years against this background of ongoing debate.

Around 1925 the Tentoonstellingsraad voor Bouwkunst en Verwante Kunsten (Council for Exhibitions on Architecture and Related Arts) was established, a joint initiative of the Vereeniging van Ambachts- en Nijverheidskunstenaars, (Association of Craft and Industrial Artists) the Bond van Nederlandse Architecten (Royal Institute of Dutch Architects), the Association Architectura et Amicitia, Kring van Beeldhouwers (Society of Sculptors) and Groep Opbouw (a discussion group for architects and artists) in Rotterdam. This Council, which later formed the basis for the Stichting Architectuurmuseum (Architectural Museum Foundation) founded in 1955, was responsible for organizing domestic and international exhibitions on architecture and visual arts with the aim of promoting Dutch art. They assembled photo panels (now part of the NAI collection) for travelling exhibitions which were in such demand that several versions were produced. The Council was also responsible for organizing the Dutch exhibit at the Exposition des Arts Décoratifs in Paris (1925) and at the world fairs in Brussels (1935) and Paris (1937).[4]

In 1923, to mark the Queen Wilhelmina's Silver Jubilee, it was decided to organize an architectural exhibition involving all the important architects of the day. These architects were subsequently asked to donate their exhibit to a future architectural museum. Evidently Leliman's idea had not yet been abandoned, despite the fact that successive commissions had so far failed to produce any tangible results. Many architects complied with the request although a few, including Michel de Klerk, refused to part with their work. Those works that were handed over formed the basis of what would later become the NAI collection. Because there was no museum building as yet, the director of the Rijksmuseum offered to store the collection for the time being in the Rijksmuseum's Print Room. The architect K.P.C. de Bazel, joint instigator and one of the driving forces behind the exhibition, bequeathed his entire archive to the future museum of architecture. This archive, like the jubilee exhibition collection, was stored for many years in the Rijksmuseum where it was eventually rediscovered in the 1960s and later added to the NAI collection.

On the eve of the outbreak of the Second World War, the idea of an architectural museum was still alive and well. To honour the architect W. Kromhout for his entire oeuvre and for his unremitting efforts to raise the standard of architecture, the sculptor Theo van Reyn was commissioned to make a bust of the architect on the occasion of his 75th birthday. On 9 May 1940, during a festive gathering at the Stedelijk Museum in Amsterdam, this bust was received on behalf of the Dutch state by Minister Bolkestein of Education, Arts and Sciences who 'gratefully accepted it for placement in the Netherlands Architecture Museum, the opening of which could however not yet be announced'.[5]

For the time being, it was to be stored at the Boijmans Museum in Rotterdam, though in fact it never arrived there owing to the outbreak of war the next day. The bust is now appropriately housed in the building of the Academie van Bouwkunst in Amsterdam, the successor to the Vereeniging voor Voortgezet en Hooger Bouwkunst Onderricht (Society for Secondary and Higher Architectural Training), the institute Kromhout had done so much to promote. His library was bequeathed to this same institute, his archive of drawings to the Royal Institute of Dutch Architects until such time as the architectural museum for which he had lobbied should be a reality.

A number of the leading architects of the day – De Bazel, Kromhout and H.P. Berlage, who also left his archive to the Royal Institute of Dutch Architects – clearly recognized the importance of such a museum. Many others were to follow them. Thus the basis of a collection for a future architectural museum was laid in the first half of the twentieth century.

In the immediate post-war period the establishment of new museums was low on the list of national priorities. The architectural profession had its hands full with reconstruction work while the government had to allocate scarce resources to more pressing issues.

It was not until 1955 that the initiative was revived. Although reconstruction work was still in full swing, people were also starting to take an interest in other matters. Once again it was architects rather than art historians or people from the museum world or government who took the initiative in founding the Stichting Architectuurmuseum (SAM). SAM accumulated a large collection but its management eventually proved to be too much for a private foundation staffed by volunteers. In the late 1960s, SAM applied to the Amsterdam city council and to central government for assistance. The city of Amsterdam responded by providing space in the peat warehouses on Waterlooplein. Central government provided financial support for the setting up of a Netherlands Documentation Centre for Architecture (NDB) to be housed in these premises. Although there was still insufficient political support for an independent architectural museum, the government did appreciate the importance of the collection of archives. The documentation centre was consequently subsumed in the Department for the Conservation of Historic Buildings and Sites. This department was also interested in post-1850 architecture and since very little was known about the architecture of this period, it was hoped that the documentation centre would help to fill this gap. Accordingly, ownership of the SAM's archives was transferred to the State and, together with the archives stored in the Rijksmuseum since the 1920s, handed over to the NDB. This was the first important, concrete step on the road to a full-fledged architectural museum.

The NDB, together with the SAM, started to organize small exhibitions around the country using material from the archives. As people got to know about the NDB, so the number of architectural archives offered to it grew. Archival research was likewise stimulated. Although the earlier initiatives had originated in architectural circles, now it was increasingly the art historians who were in the front line of efforts to give the collection a place in the Dutch cultural world. Thus the first custodian of the NDB was an art historian and the first art historical theses on the 'modern' architects De Bazel and Berlage appeared. They would be followed by many publications based on research in the collection. Rather than serving as an example of how architects might build – as the conscience of architecture, as it were – the archives became part of Dutch cultural heritage. Accordingly, the collection became in general terms an important source of information about the history of the architecture of the last two centuries.

The NDB's location on Waterlooplein seemed made to measure for an architectural museum. The Academie van Bouwkunst already had its premises there and the BNA was planning to relocate to Waterlooplein. The combination of academy, professional association and documentation centre would, it was felt, form an ideal centre for architecture and with this in mind, both the Academy and the BNA entrusted their library to the NDB, resulting in a major architectural library. It was not to be, however.

The BNA abandoned its new-build plans and it soon became apparent that the peat warehouses were in such poor condition that the NDB could not remain there; nor was there any money available for the necessary renovations. In 1974, the NDB was given alternative accommodation, also far from perfect, in a monumental government building on Droogbak where it remained until the final move to Rotterdam in 1993.

The archives continued to grow in number, size and importance (in the early 1970s Michel de Klerk's archive of drawings was rediscovered and added to the collection) and exhibition activities were expanded. In 1975, the SAM and the NDB organized highly successful architectural exhibitions in four museums across the country. The accompanying catalogues were of such high quality that they are still being consulted today. It was the first time that early 20th-century Dutch architecture had been the focus of attention on such a large scale. Interest was great and the fact that all these exhibitions could be put together from its own collection was an incentive to put even more energy into the acquisition of archives. In the course of time the accent shifted to the acquisition of the archives of architects of De Stijl and the functionalist school. This policy soon bore fruit and thanks to the NDB's ever-growing fame and good contacts in architectural circles, many major archives were acquired, including those of J. Duiker, B. Bijvoet, G. Rietveld, J.J.P. Oud, J. Wils and C. van Eesteren. With the subsequent incorporation of the archives of professional and educational organizations like the BNA and the Academie van Bouwkunst, the collection was also able to provide a good insight into the development of the architectural profession in the Netherlands. The latter acquisitions involved complete archives – not just drawings, but correspondence, photographs and models – and substantial libraries, such as the richly endowed bookshelves of Jan Wils. The publications and exhibitions organized by NDB and SAM were often the result of close collaboration with various art historical institutions.

In the long run, however, permanent under-staffing in a poorly equipped building affected the quality of these activities. This in turn finally convinced the government that it was time to find a more permanent form for the interest in architecture and urban planning than SAM and NDB alone could provide. In the meantime, another Amsterdam-based institute, Stichting Wonen (Housing Foundation), originally set up as a consumer organization aimed at propagating good-quality and sensible home furnishing, had started to operate in similar areas to NDB and SAM. It seemed logical, therefore, that these three organizations should merge. With encouragement from the ministries of Culture and Housing, who were themselves starting to show more interest in architecture and urban planning, this led to the formation of a new, private foundation, the Netherlands Architecture Institute (NAI), charged with managing the State's architectural archives. In updated form, the ideal of an architectural museum was – save for a good building – finally a reality. Once the archives the SAM had acquired since 1972 had been transferred to the State and duly handed over to the NAI to manage, all efforts were concentrated on obtaining the final piece, the building. After a fierce battle between Amsterdam and Rotterdam, the government decided in favour of Rotterdam as the site of the new building.

For the collection, the move from the old, provisional quarters in Amsterdam to the new dedicated building in Rotterdam was an enormous improvement. Thanks to a special 'removal' subsidy, it was finally possible to put the management of the collection on a professional footing and to make a start on computerization. This was urgently needed for in many cases all that was known about the contents of the 350 archives, one hundred collections, six thousand competition and exhibition panels, four hundred pieces of furniture, five hundred models, many metres of cuttings and picture postcards – some ten linear kilometres in all – was a very basic description. The libraries of the NDB and Stichting Wonen were merged and work began on a computerized access system. The move to a well-equipped repository complete with a new reading room for research demanded a systematic approach and clear access to the collection.

The basis was laid in Amsterdam, now it was Rotterdam's turn.

At long last, this unique and by now world-famous collection containing the most important products of Dutch architecture during the past two centuries, on paper and in the form of models, was installed in a new, purpose-designed building. Firmly embedded in a large organization, it now had more opportunities for development than ever before. In the new building, the various activities connected with the collection (research, services and acquisition) finally came into their own.

Research and services

The reading room for library and archival research is open to all interested persons. It provides both laymen and professionals access to an extensive, internationally-oriented library and some five hundred archives, all of which are available on request. Those engaged in intensive research – both Dutch nationals and foreigners – can apply for a space in the study centre where they can conduct their study in peace and quiet. With so many different kinds of research being carried on simultaneously by people from different parts of the world, the study centre offers a stimulating environment and encourages international exchange. The existing collaboration with universities is also continually being expanded. The ready accessibility of original material makes the NAI an invaluable research and education partner. Last but not least, research into the collection is proving increasingly useful for the NAI's own exhibition programme.

Acquisition

Up to now, acquisition has been directed towards securing complete architectural archives. Now that landscape and interior architecture have been added to the NAI's core concerns, the acquisitions policy has been extended to include these fields. For a long while, the emphasis in architecture and urban planning was on the pre-war period. But then the question arose as to whether collecting activities should also be directed at contemporary architects, and at architects' 'artwork', in order to give the collection a more museological flavour.

The appearance of a new area of research – the period of post-war reconstruction from the late 1940s to the 1970s – soon put an end to debate about where the emphasis should be laid. For the NAI, committed as it was to disseminating information about the history of Dutch architecture, the collection of material from this period, in whatever form, is perfectly logical. Moreover, researchers and policy-makers are showing more and more interest in this period. The huge post-war building production is ripe for renovation yet there is still too little information available to allow for a sound assessment of which buildings merit preservation. It is therefore vitally important that the NAI should acquire the proper sources to help researchers identify those structures that are of enduring value. This, however, raises new questions concerning what should be collected and how. There are various possibilities: all original documents (i.e. complete archives), or just a good photographic documentation of the period? Will written sources suffice (a lot has been published about reconstruction, after all), or does that give too one-sided a picture? One thing is clear, continuing to collect complete archives is out of the question. Strict selection as regards both architects and urban planners, and type of projects is an absolute must. Not only is the building production many times larger than before the war, but architectural archives, owing to different construction methods and the changing role of the architect in the building process, are a good deal more extensive than previously. Over a hundred linear metres for a single archive is no exception any more.

Nowadays the architect is more organizer than creative designer and this is reflected in the archives. Far-reaching standardization also plays a role in the debate as to what should be preserved.

Space alone would make it impossible to preserve everything, but in fact this is not necessary. More important than the pursuit of completeness is the creation of a representative survey both in the choice of architects and in a judicious selection from their oeuvre. So, with meticulous research and selection, the NAI will eventually be able to offer a well-balanced picture of both the general course and the main features of this period.

In the near future it will also be necessary to consider a question that has only arisen incidentally in the present acquisitions policy: what will a future architectural collection look like when designs are no longer worked out on paper but solely with the help of computers? Research into this aspect, including at the international level, has been slow to get going. Time is of the essence, for technological developments are so rapid that we should already be thinking about new methods of collecting and managing digitized files.

The collection from an international perspective

The International Confederation of Architectural Museums (ICAM), an umbrella organization established in 1979, comprises a great variety of architectural museums or architectural collections, all of which, however different their history and background, have the same aim: the promotion of architecture.

It is indeed a heterogeneous company: there are architectural collections that form the basis of an independent architectural museum, such as the Centre Canadien d'Architecture in Montreal, or that are integrated in museums of a more general character, such as the Museum of Modern Art in New York. Others are housed in technical universities or architectural academies (Architekturmuseum Technische Universität München), or with professional associations

(Royal Institute of British Architects, Institut Français d'Architecture), archival services and libraries, or conservation agencies (Royal Commission on the Ancient and Historical Monuments of Scotland). All these fairly diverse organizations, now numbering over eighty and scattered all over the world, together make up ICAM. In the meantime it has become clear that an architectural collection can thrive in a variety of settings. Nevertheless, the formula chosen by the NAI is regarded as a model by many other institutions.

As such the NAI occupies a special place in this wide array of organizations, even from an international perspective, not only because it has one of the largest collections in the world, but also because that collection is embedded in a broadly conceived architectural institute with multiple responsibilities, and because of the way the Dutch government has supported this Institute.

In no other country in the world does the national government have such a generous policy regarding organizations in the field of architecture and urban planning; nowhere else is a private organization like the NAI regarded as one of the partners supporting and shaping government policy. These facts are a great incentive to the NAI to strive hard to maintain this prominent position and to face the future with enthusiasm.

Mariet Willinge is Head of the Collections Department at the Netherlands Architecture Institute.

Sources

M.J. Immeker, *Voorlopige inventaris van het Nederlands Documentatiecentrum voor de Bouwkunst (1970-1988) and Stichting Architectuurmuseum (1955-1980, 1985),* Rotterdam 1993.
Annual Reports of the Department for the Preservation of Monuments and Historic Buildings, Zeist 1974-1988.

Notes

1
Verzameling bouwkundige ontwerpen bekroond en uitgegeven door de Maatschappij tot Bevordering der Bouwkunst, Amsterdam 1844-1878.
Afbeeldingen van oude bestaande gebouwen, uitgegeven door de Maatschappij tot Bevordering der Bouwkunst, Amsterdam 1854-1881, 1882-1893; 's-Gravenhage 1894-1907.
Verzameling van bekroonde ontwerpen, Architectura et Amicitia, Amsterdam 1881-1883.

2
J. Faber, B. Zwaan, *Inventaris van het archief van de Maatschappij tot Bevordering der Bouwkunst 1842-1918,* Amsterdam 1988.
J. Schilt, J. van der Werf, *Het Genootschap Architectura et Amicitia 1855-1990,* Rotterdam 1992.

3
J.H.W. Leliman, 'Een architectuurmuseum', *De Bouwwereld,* 1912, p. 345.

4
J.P. Baeten, *Inventaris/catalogus van de Tentoonstellingsraad voor Bouwkunst en Verwante Kunsten,* Rotterdam 1994.

5
I. Jager, *Willem Kromhout Czn,* Rotterdam 1992.

SchoolAtelier Activities for children and young people

SchoolAtelier is the title of a programme of activities for primary and secondary school children, organized by the Netherlands Architecture Institute throughout the school year. The aim of the programme is to stimulate interest in architecture and urban planning among school children by getting them to reflect on their immediate physical environment. They learn to look more intently at their own home, neighbourhood or city.

Primary school pupils from years 7 and 8 (aged 11–12) put themselves in the architect's shoes during workshops and guided tours where they are introduced to such concepts as 'ground plan' and 'measuring'. The programme for secondary school students consists of educational assignments related to the semi–permanent exhibition *Two centuries of architecture in the Netherlands*.

A special room in the institute – also known as the SchoolAtelier – has been set aside for school classes. Here they can work on projects involving a variety of materials such as paper, cardboard, polystyrene foam and plaster of Paris.

Primary education

For primary school pupils there is a two-part programme. First they are taken on a short guided tour of the building. This includes a peep behind the scenes of the collection where there are dozens of architectural models on display.

Next stop is the SchoolAtelier where they spend an hour and a half working on special assignments under the supervision of a member of the NAI staff. There are various materials on hand for them to use and the end products are added to the display in the SchoolAtelier. It is a fun way for children to learn what the design and construction of buildings involves. Collaboration on a single project is at the heart of the exercise.

Secondary education

The programme for secondary school students revolves around nineteenth and twentieth-century architecture. First of all an architecture student explains to them what architecture entails and how one goes about designing a building.

Then, armed with a list of questions and assignments, the students are taken around the **exhibition** *Two centuries of architecture in the Netherlands*, where they see such famous buildings as Berlage's Exchange, the Rijksmuseum and the Hilversum Town Hall. The main object is to show the students how to look at and compare buildings. For this reason, the programme includes several exercises in drawing and comparing. If desired, they may also visit the collection.

The programme anticipates the latest educational developments aimed at making students more self-reliant. It is also in line with teaching methods in visual arts subjects. Students also visit the SchoolAtelier in the context of their school studies in history (style periods) and geography (town and country planning).

Semi-permanent exhibition

Since August 1997, visitors to the NAI have been able to see an exhibition entitled *Two centuries of architecture in the Netherlands; a survey of major styles since 1800.* **This introduction to Dutch architectural history forms a fixed point in an otherwise changing programme of exhibitions in the museum. There are several ways of telling the history of architecture in the Netherlands.**

The museum has consciously opted for a conventional arrangement according to styles. This approach is not without its critics among art historians who tend to view style as a secondary aspect. For all that, a classification according to styles is almost indispensable for anyone trying to make sense of architectural history. It is only when one knows one's way around that style seems to be a minor aspect of architecture. And since the NAI's visitors include non-professionals who welcome a few guideposts, it was decided to opt for this stylistic subdivision.

Style in this exhibition is used in the traditional art historical way, as a concept of classification. It brings together related phenomena of a particular tendency, school or era under a single heading. Style is not always a clearly defined prescription but can also be used more generally to refer to a shared attitude to architecture.

The exhibition presents the key architectural works for each style and identifies the chief exponents. Occasionally, less well-known designs are included because they encapsulate the essence of a style. *Two centuries of architecture in the Netherlands* **begins with Neoclassicism, which was all the rage around 1800, and ends with Supermodernism, a designation for an approach that is emerging around the year 2000. The greater part of the material for the exhibition comes from the collection of the Netherlands Architecture Institute. As such this exhibition is**

both a concise survey of Dutch architecture and a modest cross-section of the NAI's collection.

The Netherlands Architecture Institute

Jannes Linders

p. 25, top
View of the NAI ensemble from Museumpark (south). In the middle the
pedestrian bridge to the entrance hall with above reading room, archives study
hall, library and offices, on the right the building part for exhibitions and left the
part containing collections and archives.

p. 25, bottom
View of the NAI from the east: in the foreground the pond, to the right a portion
of building part for exhibitions and behind that the part containing entrance hall,
reading room, archives study hall, library and offices.

p. 26-27
Part of the centre of Rotterdam. In the middle the NAI ensemble situated on the
edge of Museumpark.

p. 28-29
Left the arcade with the building part containing the collections and archives of
the NAI and the study centre. In the middle under the pergola, from the top
down: offices, library, reading room and archives study hall and entrance area. On
the right the tower of the Boijmans Van Beuningen Museum. In the foreground in
the pond, the sculpture by Auke de Vries.

p. 30
Corridor in the section housing the collections and archives with workrooms
above and study centre below.

p. 31, top
The NAI ensemble seen from the east. On the right the building part for
collections and archives with the arcade, on the left the part for exhibitions, in the
middle the approach to the loading zone.

p. 31, bottom
The building part containing the NAI collections and archives that defines one of
the boundaries of Museumpark.

p. 32-33
Collections and archives department with mechanically operated mobile stacks
and in the foreground two models.

p. 34
The entrance to the director's office, designed by Ben van Berkel.

p. 35
Side view: in the glass box, above the entrance area with lettering by Bruce Mau,
the reading room gallery and above that the offices. The sculpture by Auke de
Vries is visible in the background.

p. 36-37
Interior of library, reading room and archives study hall.

p. 38-39
Pedestrian bridge on the Museumpark side, one of the two entrances for the
public.

p. 40
View from the entrance hall (level 0) across the pond to the tower of the
Boijmans Van Beuningen Museum.

p. 41
The bridge leading from the entrance hall (level 0) to the ramp, lift and stairs
which provide access to all other parts of the building. The counters in the
entrance hall were designed by Bořek Šípek.

p. 42
View of balcony hall.

p. 43
Ramp linking the entrance area to the exhibition halls, library, reading room and
archives study hall.

p. 44
Interior of the main exhibition hall (with temporary exhibition on Alvar Aalto).

p. 45
Detail of the construction of the balcony hall, one of the exhibition spaces.

p. 46-47
The NAI ensemble seen from the west. Left the building part for collections and
archives, in the middle the part containing entrance hall, reading room, archives
study hall, library and offices and in the foreground in the pond, the sculpture by
Auke de Vries.

p. 48
Arcade with light sculpture.

Rode Kruis Bloedbank

aalto
... in zeven werken in seven buildings
16.5 – 16.8 1998

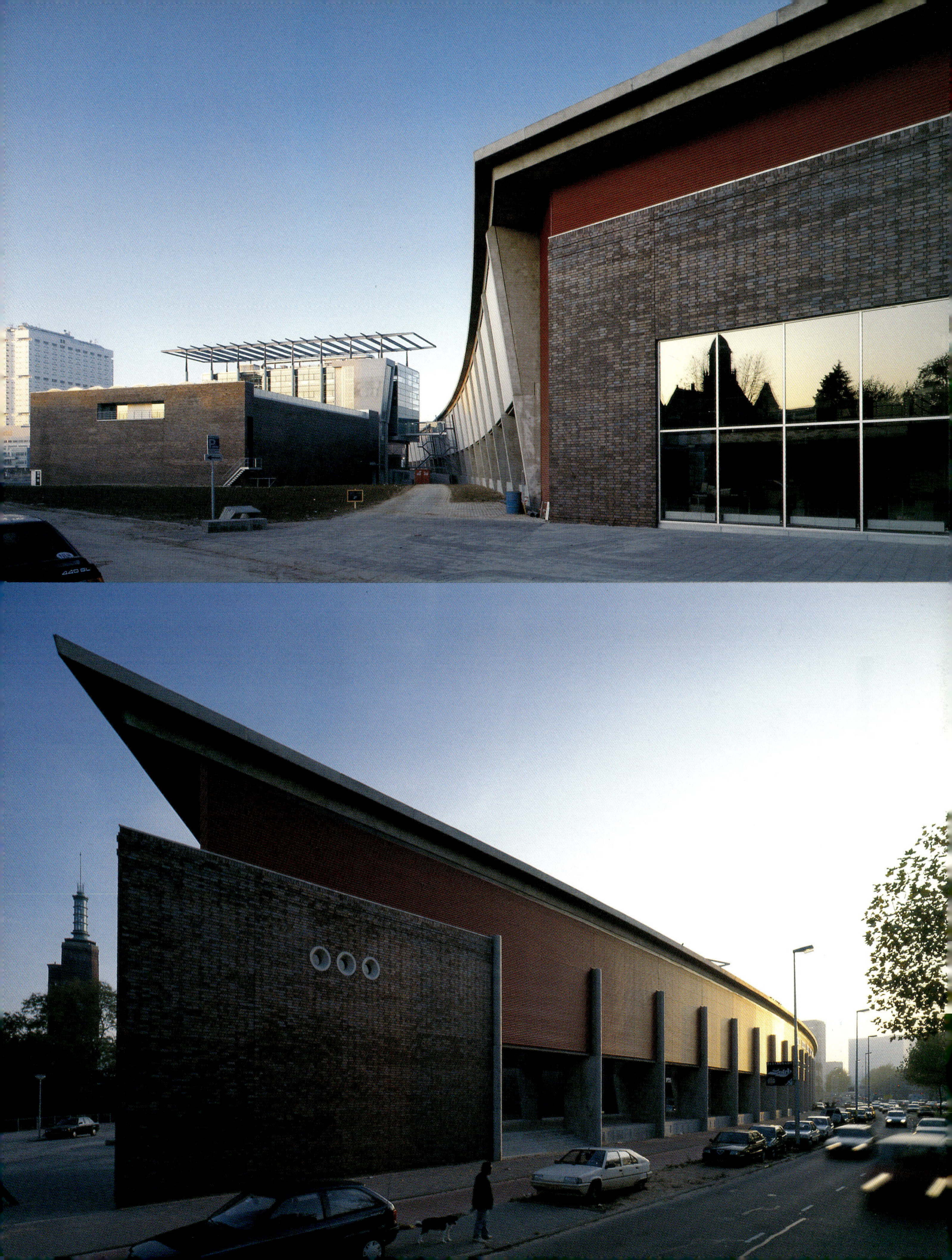

194-H-03
194-H-05
MAOV0348
Maquette - collectie
m329

Nederlands Architectuurinstituut
Kilo Boekverkopers
VVV / ArchiCenter

Inzendingen prijsvraag MoMA
MoMA competition entries

alvar
aalto
in zeven werken in seven buildings
16.5 - 16.8 1998
Nederlands Architectuurinstituut
Netherlands Architecture Institute

Site plan with NAI opposite
Museumpark and diagonally
opposite the Boijmans Van
Beuningen Museum

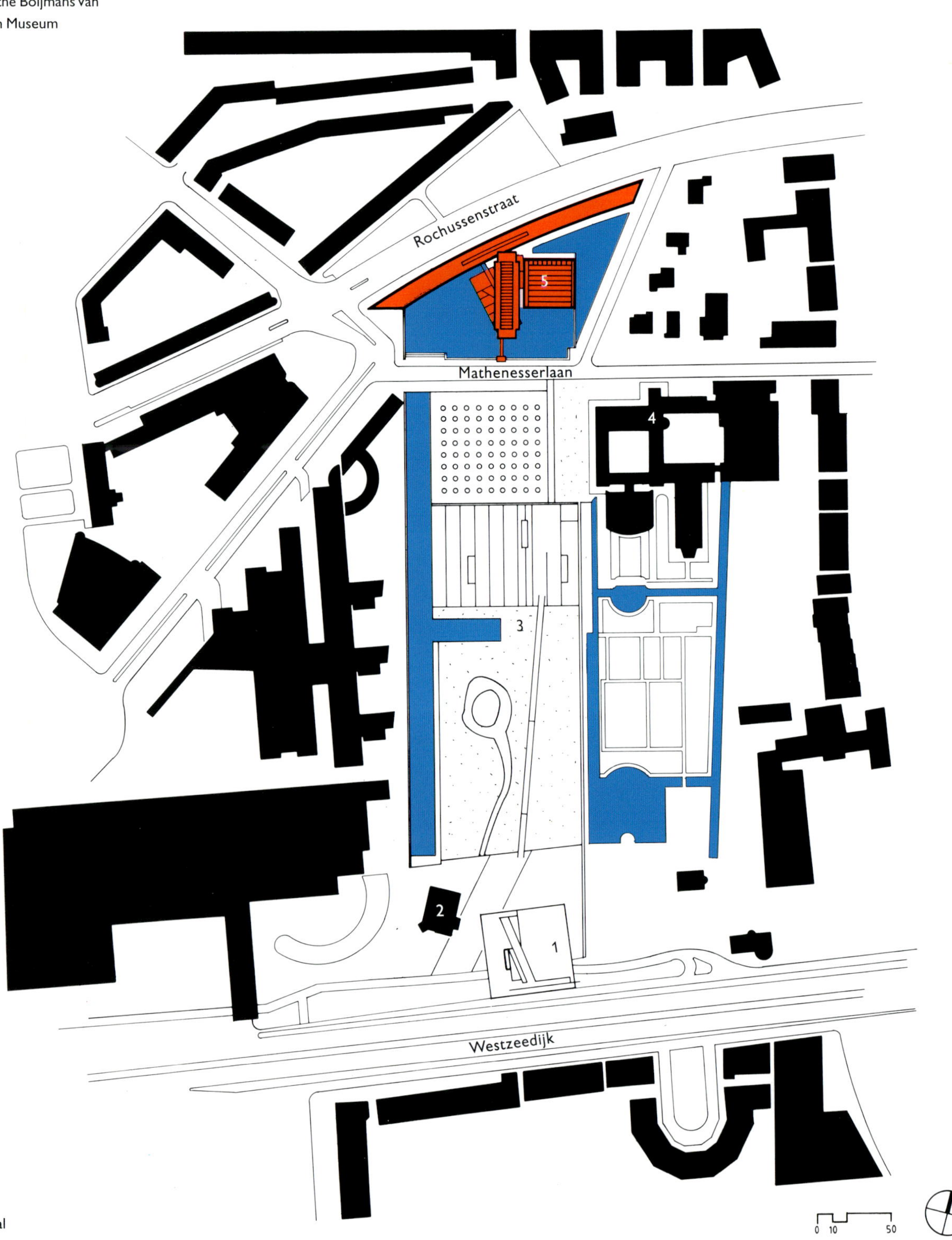

1 Kunsthal
2 Natuurmuseum
3 Museumpark
4 Museum Boijmans Van Beuningen
5 NAi

Open isometry

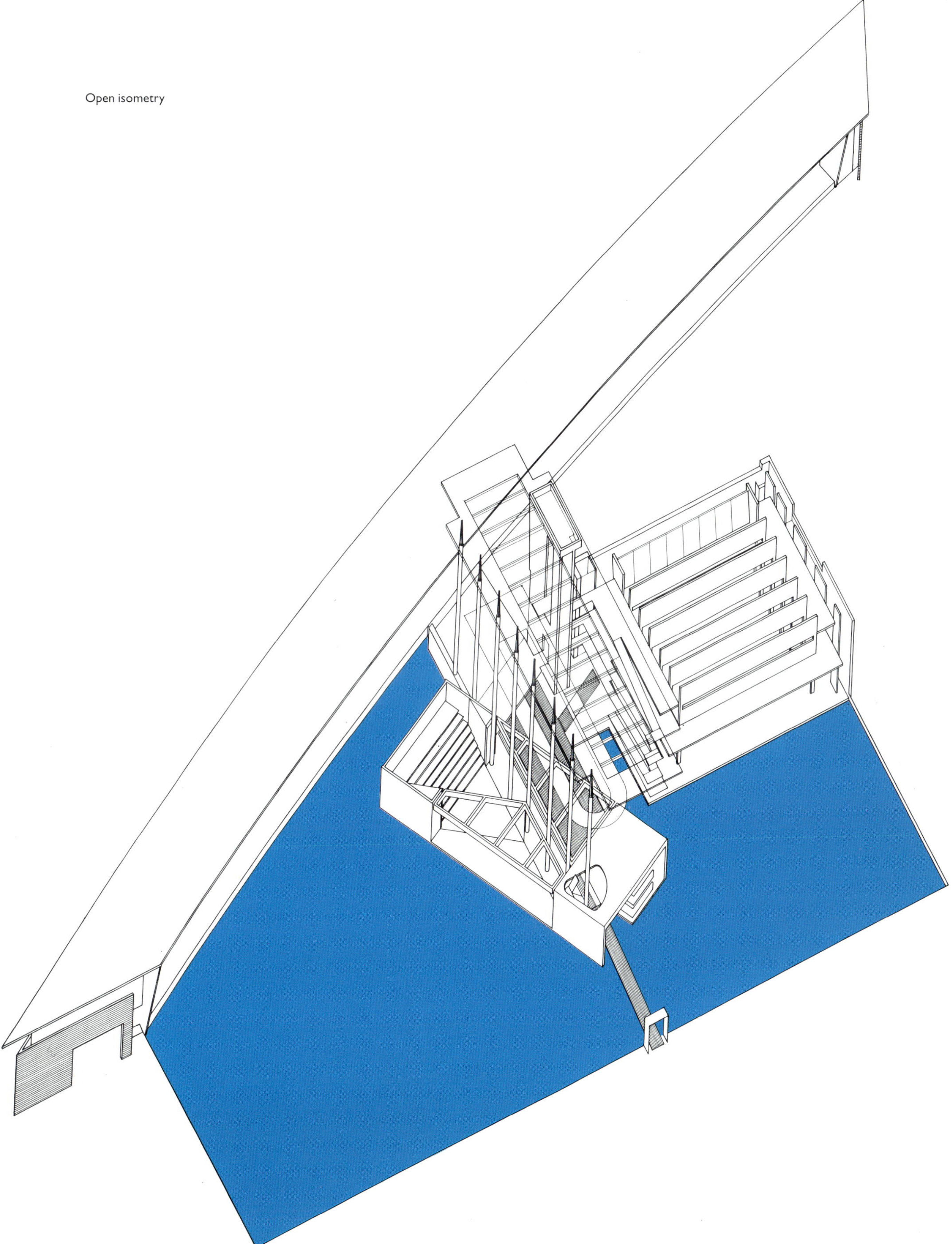

Cross section of exhibitions building; view of collections and archives part of the building above the arcade and partial view of the part with the foyer and entrance hall below, and the library, reading room and archives study hall above, as well as the office floors

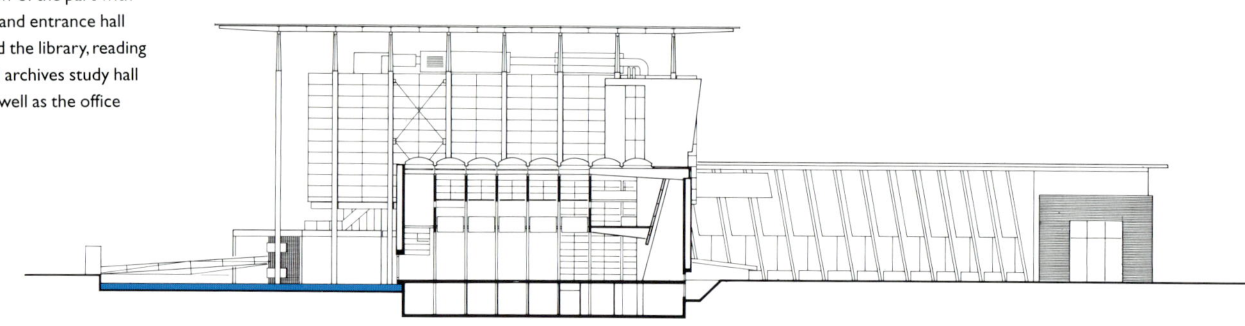

Cross section of the building part with foyer, entrance hall, two floors above with library, reading room and archives study hall and then two floors of offices; also (on the right) cross section of the arcade with above it two floors of depots (collections and archives; study centre)

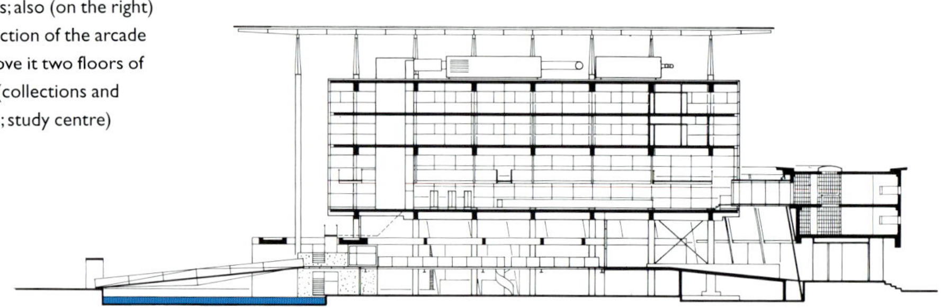

Cross section from the south (from the Museumpark side) of the building part for the exhibitions with workshops and storage under the big hall (900 m²), and of the entrance hall with under it the foyer adjacent to the auditorium and above this two floors of library, reading room and archives study hall and two floors of offices. Furthermore, a view of the building part for archives and collections above an arcade

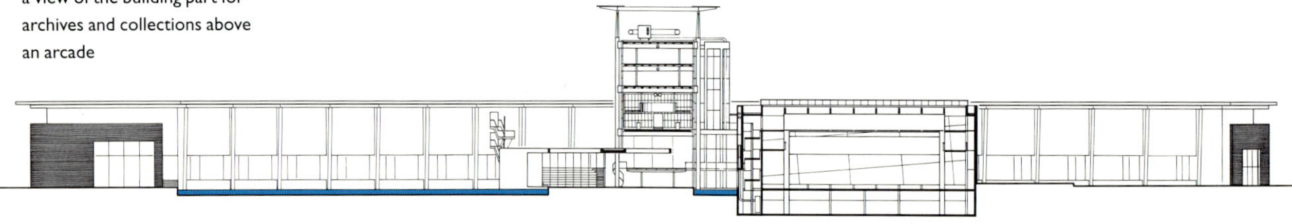

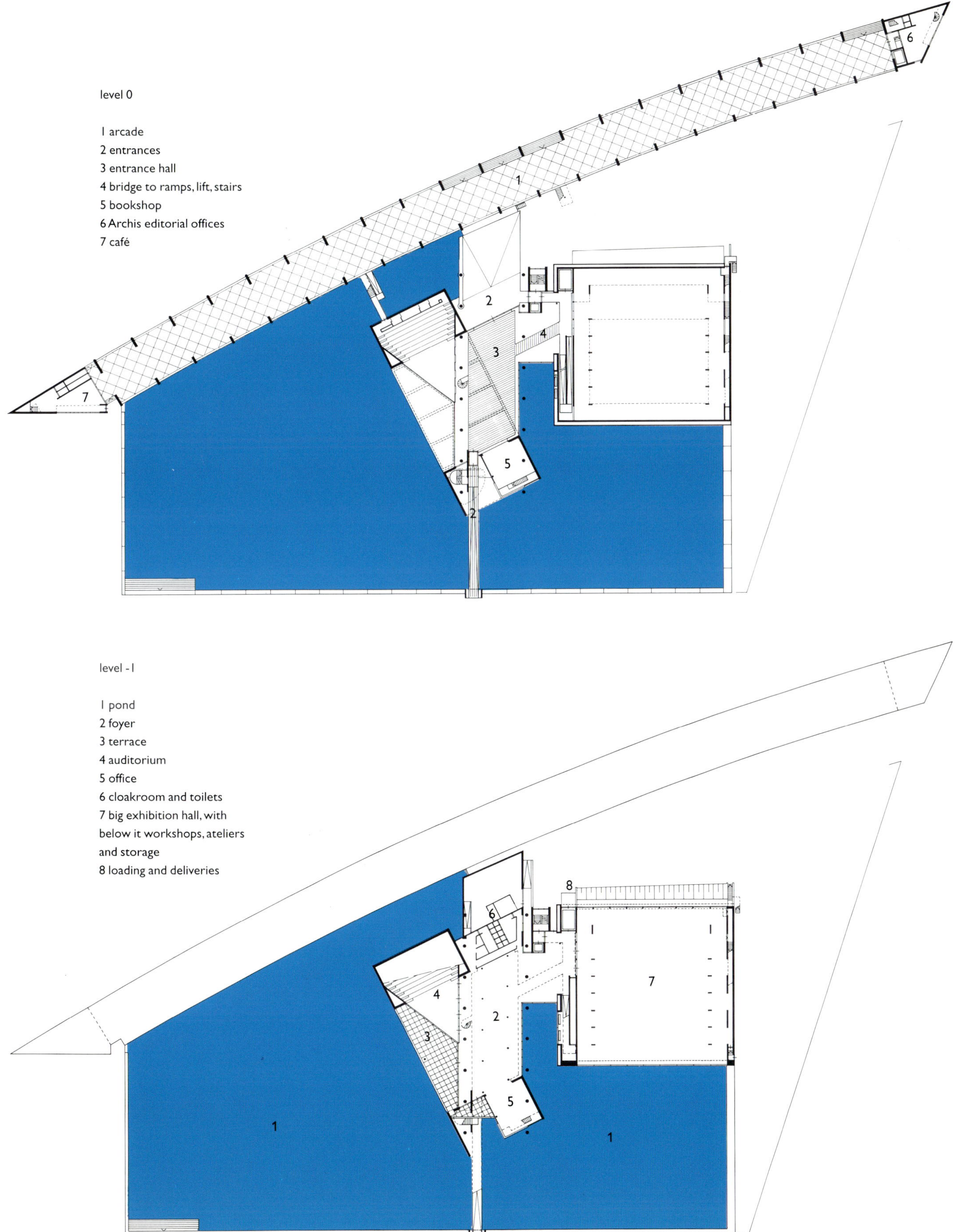

level 0

1 arcade
2 entrances
3 entrance hall
4 bridge to ramps, lift, stairs
5 bookshop
6 Archis editorial offices
7 café

level -1

1 pond
2 foyer
3 terrace
4 auditorium
5 office
6 cloakroom and toilets
7 big exhibition hall, with
below it workshops, ateliers
and storage
8 loading and deliveries

level 2

1 upper hall
2 library, reading room,
archives study hall
3 pedestrian bridge
4 work rooms for collections
and archives
5 depots collections and
archives

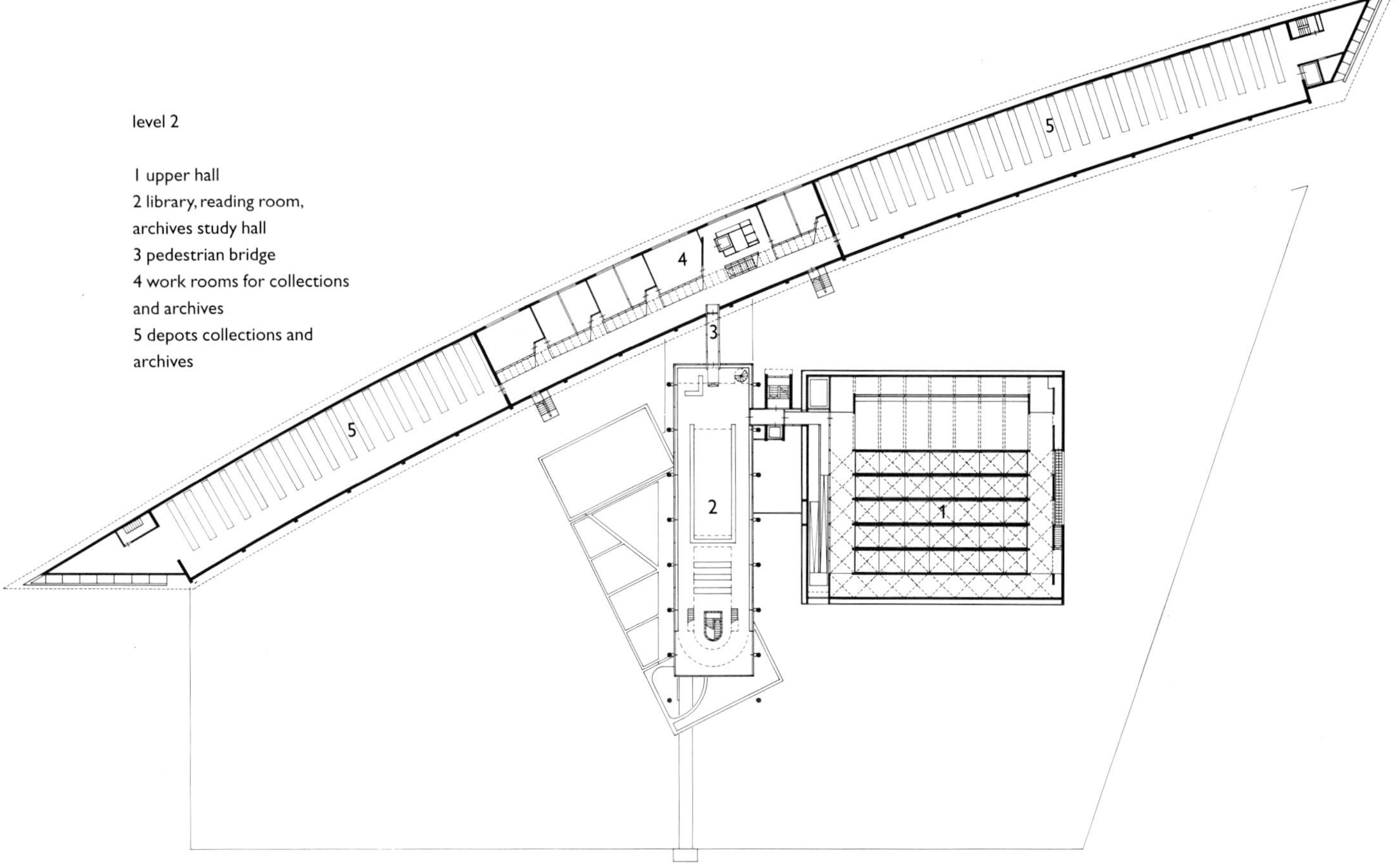

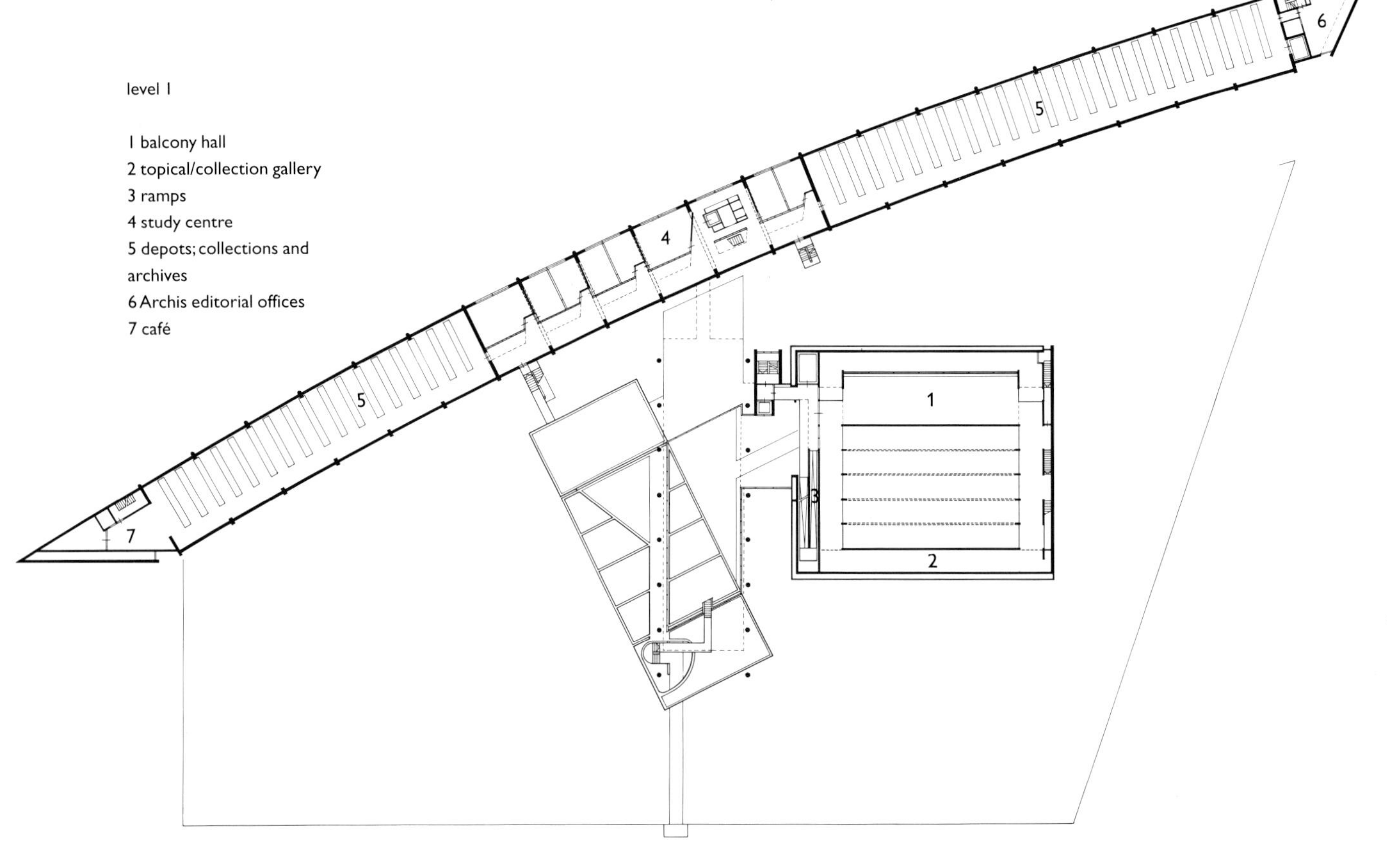

level 1

1 balcony hall
2 topical/collection gallery
3 ramps
4 study centre
5 depots; collections and
archives
6 Archis editorial offices
7 café

level 4 + 5

1 offices
2 boardroom
3 director's study cum
conference room

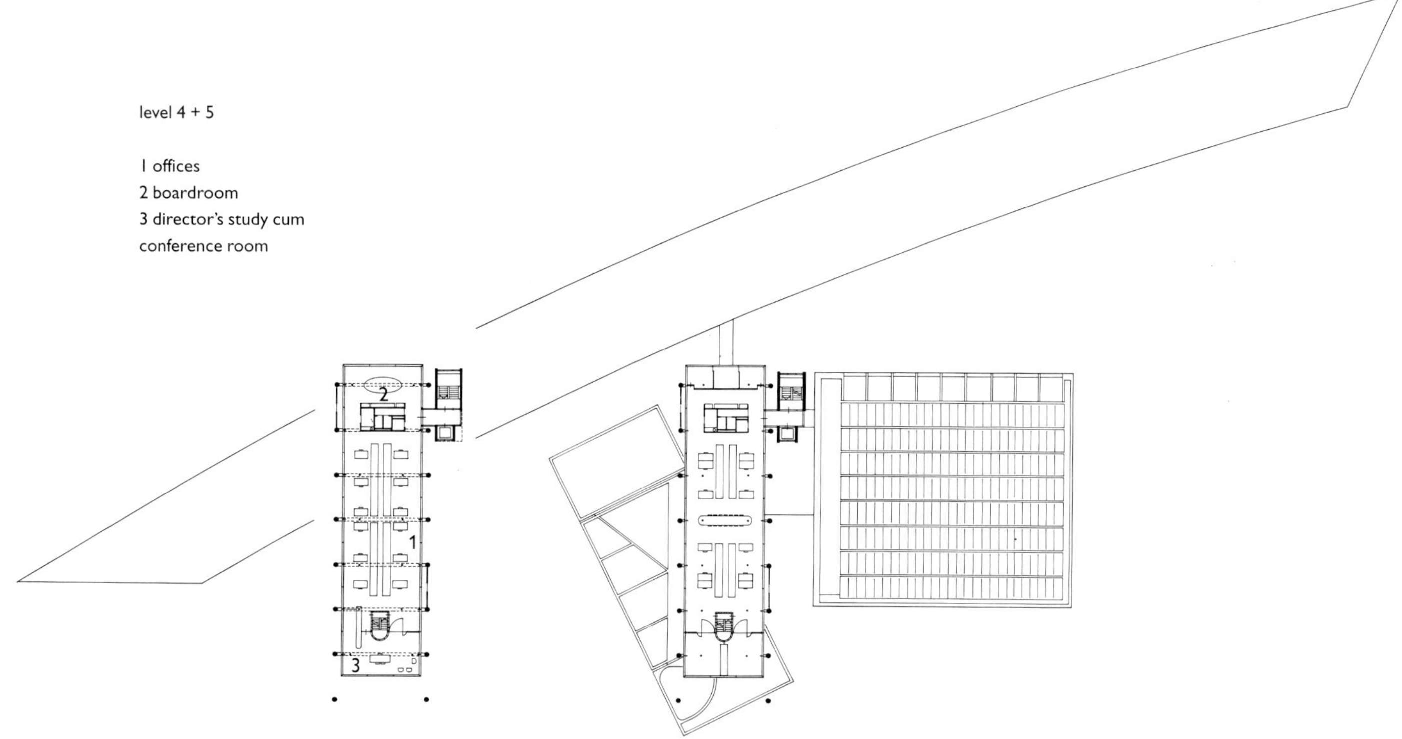

level 3

1 upper gallery library

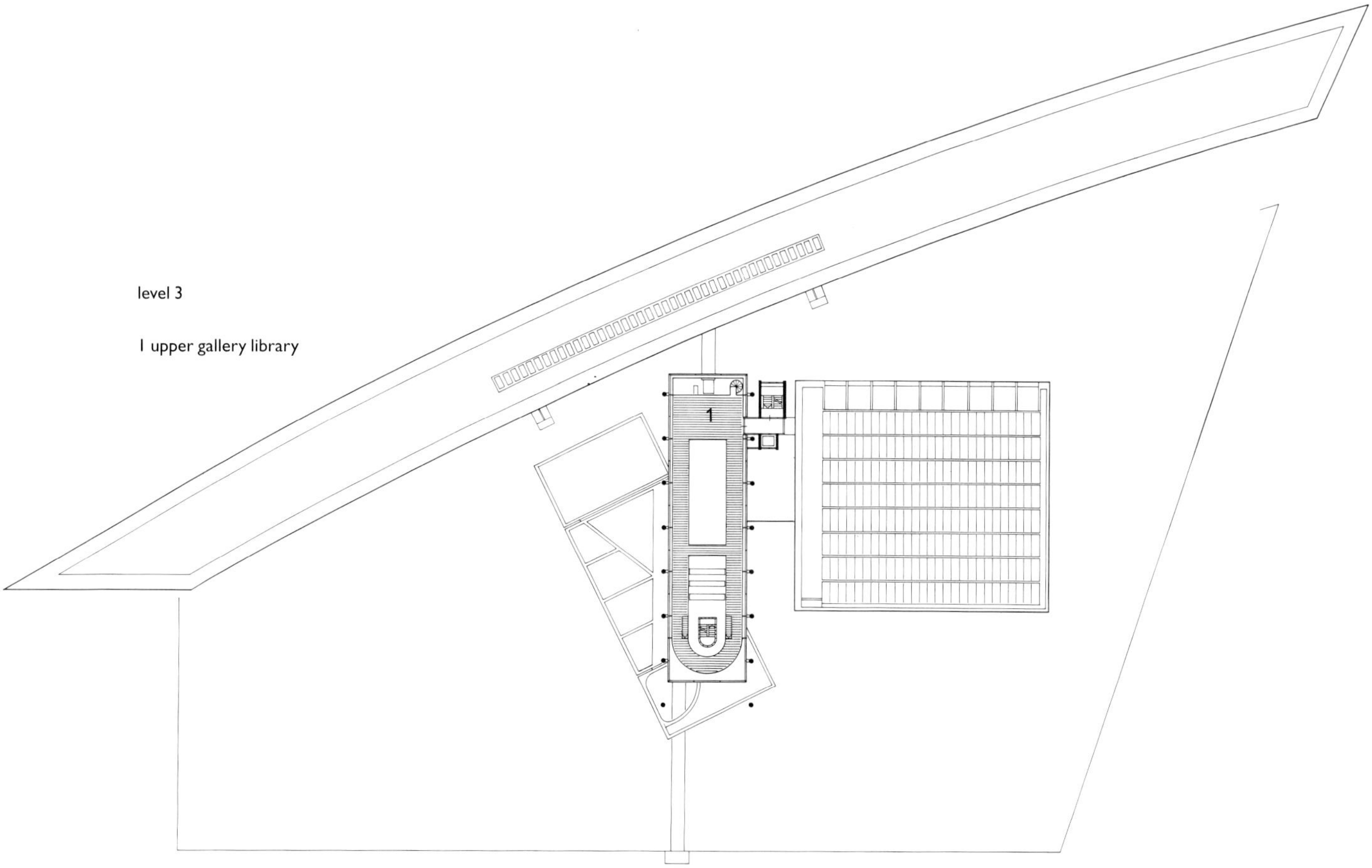

Project information

Architect: Jo Coenen & Co Architecten bv, Maastricht/Eindhoven
Design: Jo Coenen
Period: 1988-1993

Commissioned by: Netherlands Architecture Institute

Building management, site manager: Ingenieursbureau
Grabowsky & Poort bv

Building contractor: Strukton Bouwprojekten bv
Installations: GTI Rotterdam Cappelle bv

Pond and site contractor: G.A. van Dijk & Zn nv

Consultants for:
Construction: Advies- en Ingenieursburo Van de Laar bv
Installations: Projektservice Dynatherm Zuid bv
Sprinkler installation: bv Technisch Inspectie- en Adviesbureau Nagtglas
Versteeg
Lighting for exhibitions building section: Lightdesign Ingenieursgesellschaft MBH
Acoustics: Adviesbureau Peutz & Associes bv
Museum conditions: Centraal Laboratorium voor Onderzoek van
Voorwerpen van Kunst en Wetenschap

Artists:
Light artwork in arcade: Peter Struycken; Neomat United Laboratories
Sculpture in pond: Auke de Vries

Other designers:
Structural loadbearing glass walls of entrance hall and foyer:
Mick Eekhout, Octatube Engeneering bv and Octatube Space Structures bv

Counters of entrance hall, furnishing of foyer and auditorium lectern: Bořek Šipek

Interior of director's office cum conference room: Ben van Berkel

Interior lettering: BRS Premsela Vonk

Exterior lettering: Bruce Mau

Fittings for offices, reading room, archive study hall: USM-Haller

Costs
Building: 31,8 million guilders
Furnishing: 5,2 million guilders

Complex but uncomplicated

Jo Coenen

The NAI consists of building sections arranged spatially to form an ensemble in the urban landscape. The architectural unity between the various sections is a function of their mutual relationship: the fragments work as a whole.

The entrance hall forms a route which links up with the Museumpark. From this hall the visitor can reach all the important spaces in the Institute. During opening hours this route makes the building part of the public space.

Once inside, the visitor can simply cross the foyer and exit again on the other side or take another route, from one part of the building to another. The rich variation of places and experiences which have their own place in this building, make a walk through the complex an exciting experience.

The basic principle is simple. The four building sections represent the four functions: entrance hall with foyer and auditorium, museum (exhibition halls), archives and library-reading room with offices above. Each function has been expressed on the exterior by using a different material. The museum – the exhibition halls – is clad in brick, the archives building in steel plate. The main building is of glass and, like the plinth building, allows the concrete load-bearing structure behind it to be seen. Due to the tight budget and the desire for plainness, the skeleton has been elaborated in such a way that it also functions in enclosing space. The load-bearing structure and the pipes are nakedly shown alongside each other.

The programme components are linked in such a way that not only is an efficient and rapid working process guaranteed, but they are also able to complement one other in meaning. The pond plays an important role in this as partition, link and mirror. The giant sculpture by Auke de Vries fits wonderfully into this. The long archives building, constructed on 42 columns,

is also a covered street, an arcade, which gives access to the complex. This building section both borders and provides access to the Museumpark. In the evening it is festively illuminated by computer-controlled coloured lights that produce a rainbow effect. Thanks to Peter Struycken's artwork, the building is also in tune with the Rotterdam atmosphere at night.

The loadbearing construction of the glass main building has a dual purpose. It supports the building section and also, by virtue of the pergola construction, acts as an eye-catching sign that announces from afar the presence of this important urban park area. Pragmatism and symbolism both play a role and alternate with each other where there was a reason to do so in the design.

Because of the way in which the plan is composed of parts there are unexpected vistas and views of water and greenery from various angles. This scene-setting game produces alternating atmospheres in the building, with inner and outer domains. From one section, you look back at the other.

The rooms succeed one other as in a series: from a light hallway you enter an immense hall; narrow ramps bring you to a high circulation gallery with an elegant balcony hall and a severe gallery. Higher still is the attic hall, the roof with joists forming parallel spaces.

The exhibitions box is made up of specific spaces which, like the building sections, are prototypes, even though the overlaps mean that they will not immediately be recognized as such. As a result of the recurrent use of concrete for the walls, the structure and the repeated dimensions, a coherent image is created in which none of the elements is emphasized or is more in the foreground. Inside the structure, the voids and openings through which light enters produce an exuberant spatial game which remains subdued because of the restricted use of materials. From the outside, only traces of this can be seen through the sparingly cut apertures. The surprise effect is increased by application of the specially fired bricks from northern Germany. Strong sunlight turns the museum building into a luminous box against a green background; in bad weather the building looks sombre, standing there like some mysterious and heavy mass.

The ensemble is anchored in the city and also in the Museumpark which is part of the city. The edges of the water and of the greenery near the building form a channel on the Museumpark side which marks off the domain of the NAI. The bridge over the water has a concrete portal which catches the eye of the park visitor from a distance. Once inside the entrance hall, a wooden bridge takes the visitor to all parts of the complex.

The use of material is restrained. The concrete skeleton dominates the picture, complemented by steel, glass, wood and brickwork. The limited budget made it necessary to have the most impressive skeleton possible, which can later be filled in with precious materials. One such addition is already in place: the USM-Haller furniture in the library and the offices. Like the construction and composition of the main building, the furniture developed by Fritz Haller is systematic and pragmatic, and it fits in perfectly with the design of this building section.

I think I can point to a number of related series of designs in my work. While earlier works like the Heerlen library, the Eindhoven health centre and Pizza Bun in Almere, all built around 1984, were based on the theme of the central hall space, in this plan the spatial concept explodes, shooting out freely on all sides. The designs of three more recent works are based on this last approach: the NAI in Rotterdam, the arts cluster in Tilburg and the Kulturforum in Offenburg. All three were made within a short space of time. As if by way of dress rehearsal, they were preceded by the realization of the

villa and office building for Haans in Tilburg. Apart from the obvious points of resemblance between the Haans offices and the NAI – similar roof construction, tall and slender columns, transparent glass walls and pond – they have the same architectural-urbanist theme: the careful arrangement of building sections in the surroundings. This theme has been used throughout the history of architecture (from the Islamic Taj Mahal to the modern Chandigarh by Le Corbusier) to lend buildings a certain significance and symbolic value. For my part, I was also interested in achieving an uncomplicated naturalness.

A number of designs for building complexes have inspired me to make urban configurations. They are the plans for the Dominican convent in Media by Louis Kahn, for the German embassy in Rome by Oswald Mathias Ungers and for the Wissenschaftszentrum in Berlin by James Stirling. The last plan was not built entirely as originally designed, the other two were never built. The singular configurations they reveal have sources of inspiration in the distant past. The Hadriana Villa in Tivoli, the Campo Santo in Pisa and the *collage plans* for Roman and late Renaissance buildings noted by Colin Rowe are all ensembles. They are based on coincidences and apparent contradictions which are incorporated into the basic plan. I was struck by the wealth of different types of space and the precision of the boundaries. This is also true of the castles along the Loire and of Hoensbroek castle in my native region where, after negotiating a magnificent series of portals, bridges over ponds and canals and courtyards, past stereotypical buildings, a sharp turn finally brings one to the *belly* of the main building. Some mining complexes also reveal a surprising sequence of diverse buildings. They are a permanent source of inspiration for me.

In the three plans mentioned for Rotterdam, Tilburg and Offenberg the free arrangement of the volumes goes hand in hand with a precise anchoring in the surrounding landscape. The existing surroundings become the basis for the

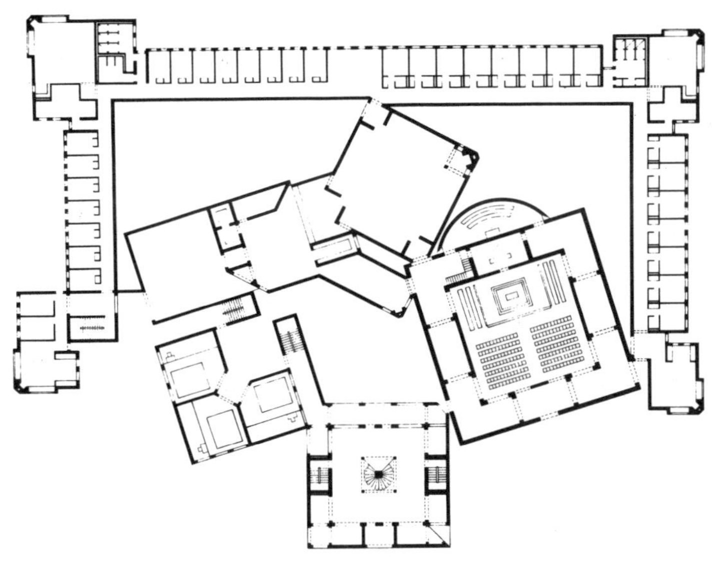
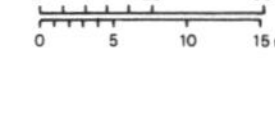

Unbuilt design by Louis Kahn
for a Dominican monastery in
Media, Pennsylvania, USA,
1965-1968

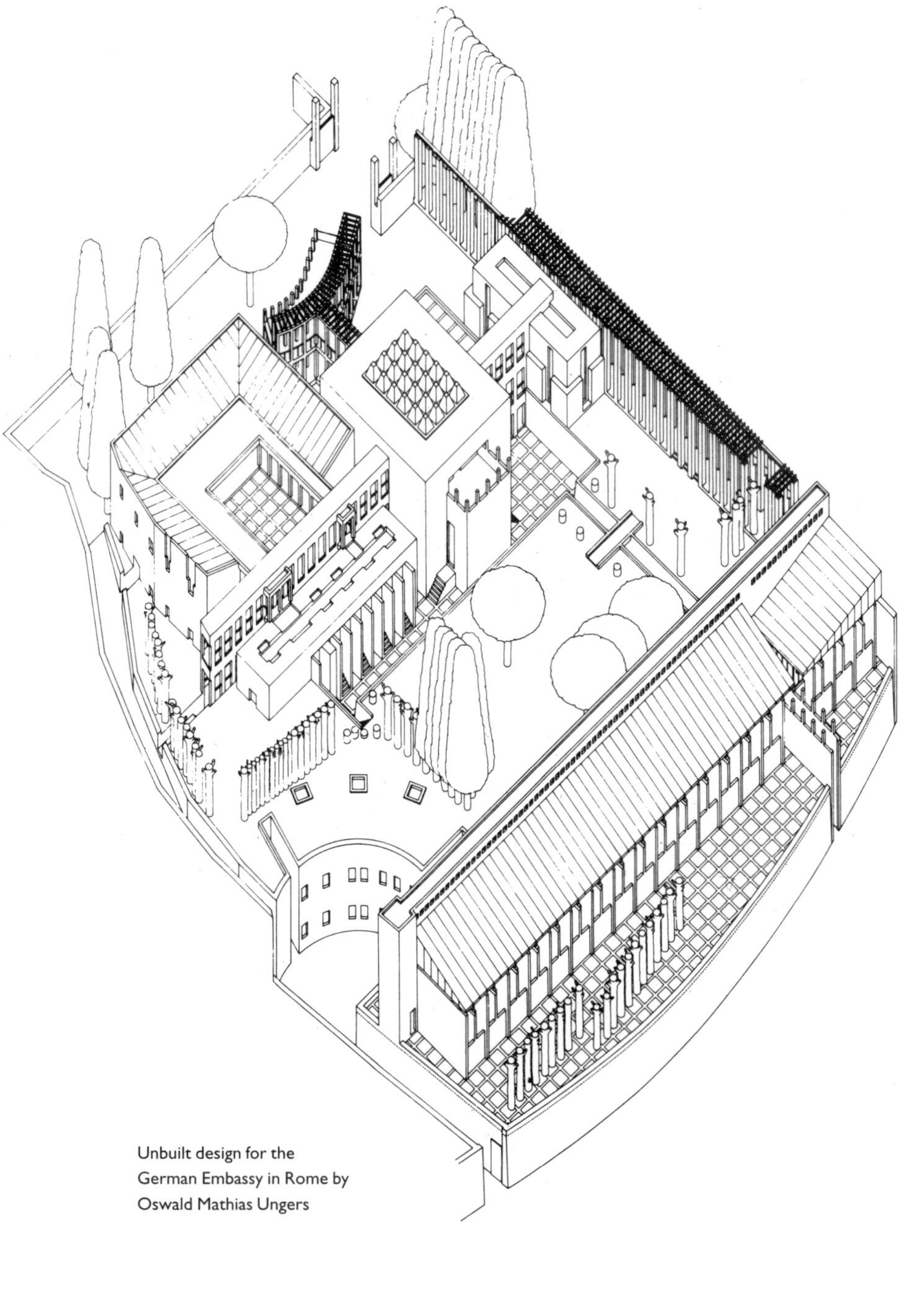

Unbuilt design for the
German Embassy in Rome by
Oswald Mathias Ungers

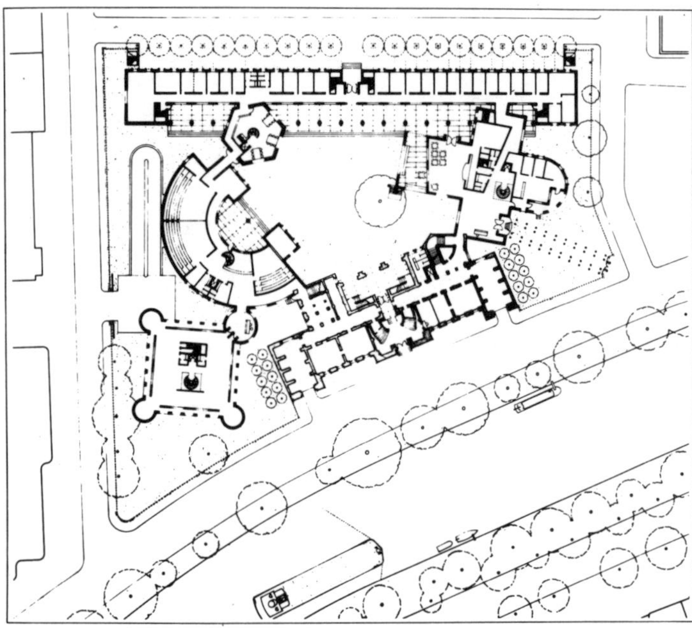

Floor plan of the Sciences
centre in Berlin; not built
completely as designed by
James Stirling, 1979

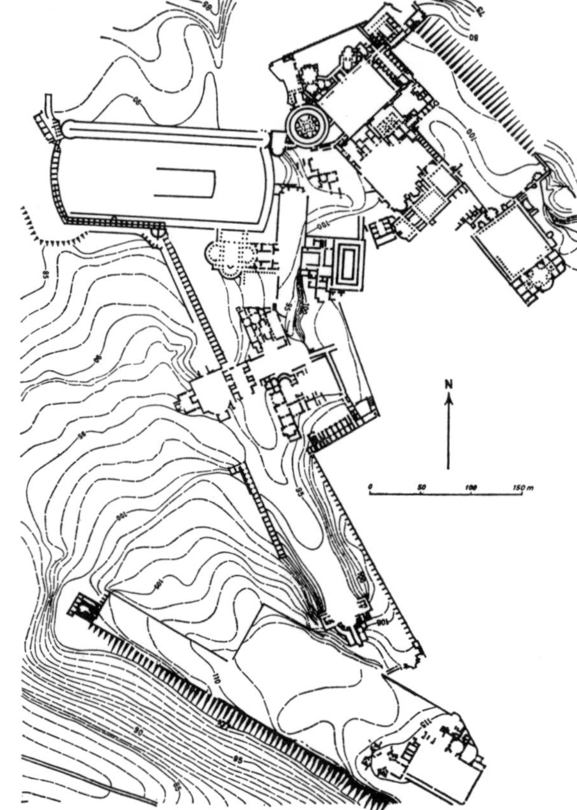

Floor plan Villa Hadriana, Tivoli

Travel sketch by Le Corbusier
of the Campo Santo (Piazza
dei Miracoli), Pisa, 1911

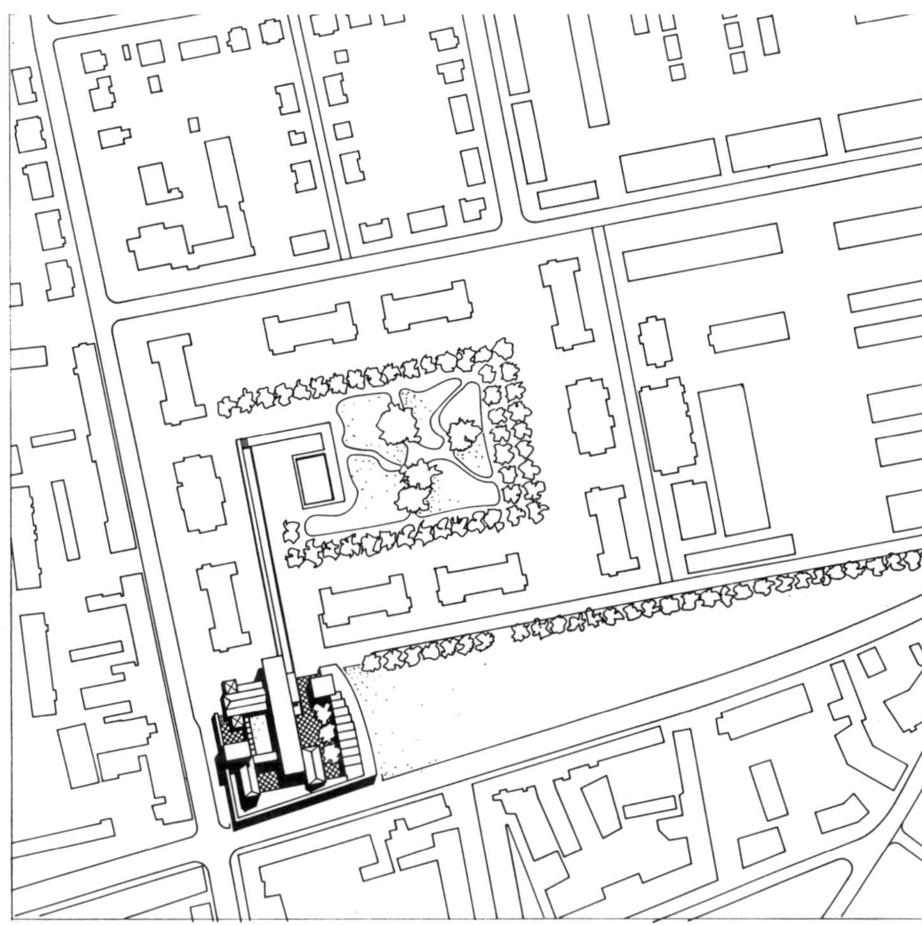

Cultural Centre Offenburg, Germany. Floor plan and site plan. Design Jo Coenen

design work. The complex is etched into them and elaborated into a domain. It complements and enriches the environment. The anchoring is sometimes done through the building sections, but also through more natural elements; it can extend far into the surroundings, but also, in highly compressed form, cover a small area. Exhibitions building, steps, landings, bridges and terraces are devices linking the complex to the public domain.

The complex has walls, but they are not definitive boundaries: exterior includes interior, and interior includes exterior, areas flow into each other. The building acquires a pragmatic and a narrative expression: the expression of an organization as public institution. As well as naturalness, the everyday is also accorded dignity, a kind of presence. The urban

configuration makes the building part of a larger whole. The characteristic of a spot is reinforced; the building actually turns it into a new spot with, once again, its own distinctive character.

While in Rotterdam's Museumpark the context for the free play with building segments is found in urban and natural elements, such as garden and pond walls, steps, doorway, bridge and the long arcade, in Tilburg the free forms are tied together by a broad ribbon to form a square. This square building is among a series of striking buildings along the Schouwburgring in the centre of the city and defines the gap between theatre and monastery both as the entrance to the College of Arts and as the gateway to the splendid monastery garden, which is bordered by the new buildings of the arts cluster. Ranged around a public courtyard are the public elements of the arts cluster: the foyer, the cafe, the media library and the assembly hall of the arts faculty. Beside this is the route of raked passageways leading up to the city's raised Music Theatre. This public space, the city foyer, will become the distribution point between city and building, a place where everybody can hang round.

In the plan for the Kulturforum in Offenburg the ground plan takes its cue from all the existing buildings and directions. Connecting lines are laid deep into the surroundings. The framing and anchoring, which is largely abandoned in this plan, are confined to a single side of the complex. In this plan too it is above all the infrastructure that dictates the placing of spaces and their size and access. The visitors' route through the complex is the main theme. Through portals and openings in the walls, they arrive at courtyards which in turn act as a conduit to foyer, corridors, stairs and ramps, leading on to the halls, cafe and schools. The various building parts are stacked, apparently at random, alongside and on top of one other and express a high degree of simplicity. The incorporation and manipulation of existing buildings, in combination with the arrangement of the new blocks around this, is a useful motif for building a city in miniature.

Although it would be going too far to call my approach methical, the same working methods can be found in each of the projects. First of all the infrastructure of the planning area is picked up, the lines along which the boundaries and the movements are projected.

Then, there are one or more visual characteristics and associations which fix the mood, the contours and the arrangement of the spaces.

The working method could even be called primitive. Starting from the questions 'what is there, what can I do with it and what needs to be made?', all conceivable data – not only the historical – are incorporated into the plan.

The combination of answers produces a spatial context, within which the game of scene-setting can begin. After all, buildings carry both many colours and many meanings, can be imposing and stately, but also informal, uncomplicated, and convenient to use. They are at their best when they are not too definitive and leave room to manoeuvre.

As a city grows in configurations from small to large, so too these concepts of a building, both in their entirety and in their small components, are narratives which assimilate the specific character of the city and the spot. In their main structure, the plans remain clear and simple, becoming multiform and complex where they touch the ground, absorbing everything they encounter along the way. They always create a new environment.

Cultural Centre Offenburg,
Germany. Sketch of
perspective. Design Jo Coenen

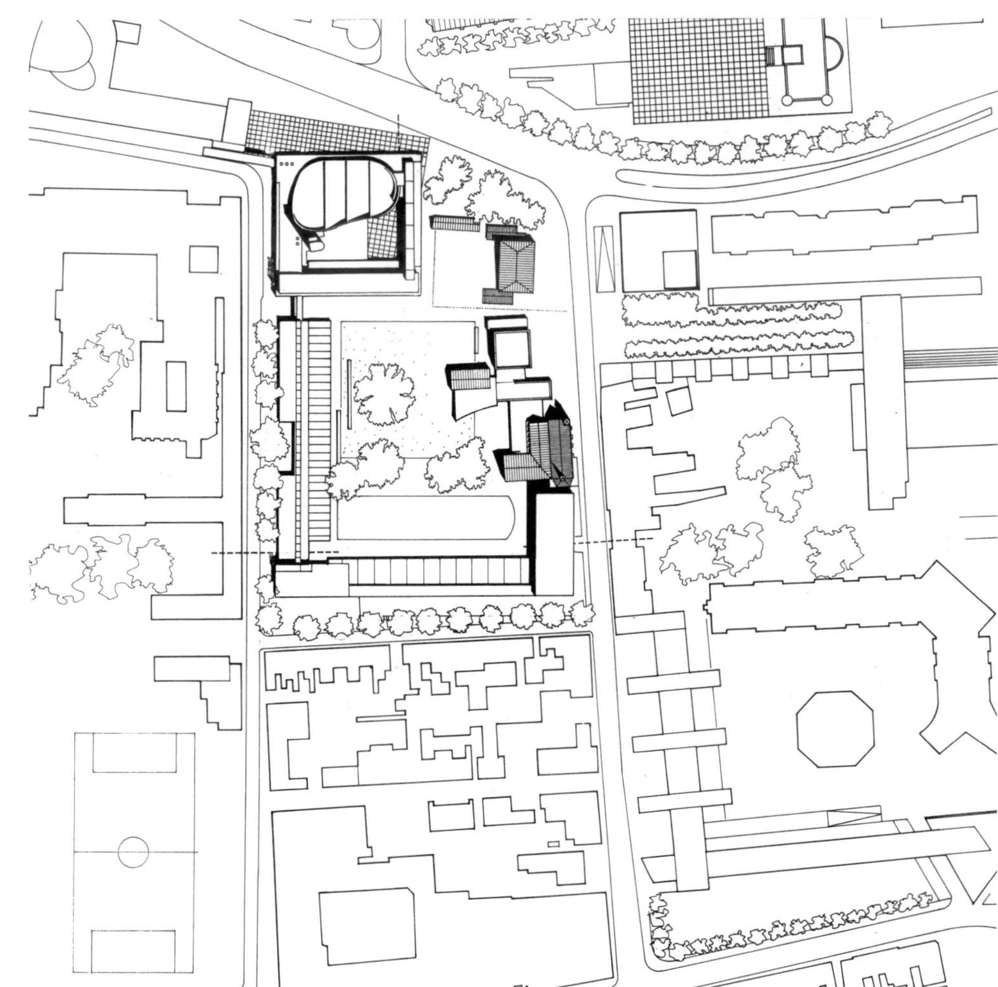

Arts cluster Tilburg;
floor plan and site plan.
Design Jo Coenen

The NAI — the history of a design task

Ruud Brouwers

Originally, it was not at all the intention that the Netherlands Architecture Institute (NAI) should get a new building, and certainly not in Rotterdam. For the NAI in the making in the mid-1980s the shining prospect was Berlage's Beurs in Amsterdam. A large part of this building had been offered by the capital's city council. User studies from 1985 by the architects Benthem Crouwel among others, showed that the institute would fit well into it. Nevertheless, on 29 February 1992 the Minister of Health, Welfare and Culture (WVC), Hedy d'Ancona, officially drove in the first pile for the new building in the Museumpark in Rotterdam, whose doors would be thrown open to the public in the autumn of 1993. On this leap year day she was assisted by representatives of various other government departments who were co-financing the project. For although the NAI is a private foundation, it is tied to the subsidizing state by golden cords. Furthermore, it manages impressive collections and archives – sketches, drawings, maquettes, documents, books and journals – which for the most part belong to the state. So despite its formal status as an independent 'national museum', the NAI was not free to choose where it would be located.

This most recent in a long line of attempts to found an architecture museum in the Netherlands almost ran aground on the question of the location. Without the financial cooperation of the Ministry of WVC in particular it was not possible to found the NAI. Yet acceptance of this cooperation brought with it the inexorable condition of locating in Rotterdam. The initiators had nothing against Rotterdam, but they viewed this condition as an unjustified and mistaken move away from Amsterdam, as an infringement of independence and as a heavy mortgage. A location in the middle of Amsterdam would, unlike the Rotterdam site, have guaranteed high visitor numbers with a favourable prospect for the future running of the institute.

The history of the collections and archives that the NAI manages, augments and makes accessible to the public is a separate story. This is a brief account of the new building that was built to a design by Jo Coenen. Nevertheless, something of the prior history needs to be related here, for the NAI and with it the new building did not simply appear out of thin air. Why it should suddenly have been possible to set up the NAI in the late 1980s when all earlier attempts to establish a national architectural museum had come to naught, is difficult to explain in terms of cause and effect. Evidently the right people were in the right places and the climate was finally favourable. Post-war rationalism, owing to the continuing big demand for new buildings (an acute housing shortage and the transformation of the Netherlands into a modern industrial and trading nation) and the institutional character of construction in the Netherlands, enjoyed a long and tenacious life. In the 1970s, nevertheless, a thorough reorientation took place, nourished by a variety of sources: a growing aversion to monotonous uniformity, the rediscovery through urban renewal projects of the significance of the urban fabric and a positive assessment of spectacular architecture abroad. This correction of a technocratic, arid modernism was characterized by a revived interest in architectural history and the design process. Architecture was rediscovered as an area of knowledge with a history, theory and practice of its own. In national cultural policy, 'architecture' was accorded a prominent place alongside the visual arts for example. The tangible results of this new perspective have been a government policy geared to stimulating architecture and urban planning through special funds and advisory bodies, and the subsidies for the NAI.

The development roughly outlined here meant a growing interest in the collections and archives of private designers from the nineteenth and twentieth centuries in the Netherlands Architectural Documentation Centre (NDB). This centre had been set up in 1972 as a branch of the Historic Buildings Service (a department of the C-section of the Ministry of WVC) to run all the treasures which had been collected up to then. On this occasion the Architecture Museum Foundation (SAM) donated its property to the state. Founded in 1955, the SAM was the latest in a long line of initiatives to create an architecture museum, with roots going back beyond the middle of the nineteenth century. Apart from facilitating research aimed at protecting more recent architecture, providing loans and participating in projects of diverse museums, the staff of the NDB, together with active board members of the SAM, began to hold exhibitions themselves in the rather inaccessible building they shared with other government institutions on the Droogbak in Amsterdam.

Barely two kilometres from the Droogbak, Stichting Wonen was doing the same with state subsidy in shop premises on the Leidsestraat. Originally founded to provide information in the field of housing, culturally-oriented educational work intended to allow consumers to profit fully from a modern dwelling by means of practical furnishing at a reasonable price, the focus had shifted to giving a voice to action groups in the urban renewal areas. Its agenda was dictated by topical urban controversies. Nevertheless the focus was directed to architecture and the role and position of architects in the building process. The problems of urban renewal and land use automatically entailed an exploration of the history of architecture and town planning. Little by little, the paths of the staff of the NDB and of Stichting Wonen began to cross each other in the inner city of Amsterdam, with regard to use of the collections, cooperation with architects and architectural historians and the making of exhibitions and publications.

At the beginning of the 1980s the NDB and Stichting Wonen even began to look around for shared accommodation in Amsterdam, to replace the 'shoe box' on the Leidsestraat and the building on the Droogbak, which was unsuitable for the proper administration of the collections and archives. The discussions with regard to the founding of a fully-fledged architecture institute also continued, the question being whether Stichting Wonen would be allowed to collaborate on this, considering the group's somewhat unruly background. In 1983 the then minister of WVC, Elco Brinkman, made it known that he wanted to investigate how the state might contribute to the creation of the desired museum. At his invitation, a five-party consultation got underway in early 1984, with representatives of both the housing and culture ministries, the NDB, SAM, and Stichting Wonen. In the background, Jan Jessurun played a driving role, first in his position as head of the Historic Buildings Service, later as deputy director-general for culture. With his preference for a multi-coloured open society, he pushed the NAI in the direction of a non-official institution which is free to express opinions and fulfil a critical role. Very aptly, it was Jessurun who, on 7 January 1993, set off the fireworks to celebrate the topping-out of the NAI building.

Before the end of 1984 the five party consultation finished their work with the *White Paper, design for a Netherlands institute for architecture and town planning.* The word design does not stand for any form of architecture, but for a structure with regard to content and organization. The paper was accompanied by a recommendation from both the official camp and the institutions involved, to the ministers for housing and culture, that the institute be established in Berlage's Beurs in Amsterdam. The Rotterdam city council had already offered the building of the former library and reading room on Nieuwmarkt and Botersloot (1923, architect D.B. Logeman, in collaboration with N. Lansdorp and J. Poot) as accommodation for the NAI, with the urgent request to the ministers to designate Rotterdam as the location. The state's neglect of this city in the allocation of funds for culture was proffered as an argument in favour of Rotterdam. As a gesture, Rotterdam had Rem Koolhaas design a conversion and extension of the old library building.

On the basis of the policy document, the minister, Elco Brinkman, saw in an architecture institute a sword that could cut both ways. In line with the significance of architecture in society, a fully-fledged cultural institution could be created, a suitable and above all safe accommodation for the valuable collections and archives. At the same time, it offered the possibility of finally giving Rotterdam a museum subsidized by the state, that would also fit in with municipal cultural policy which emphasized applied arts like photography, everyday objects and architecture. A considerable part of Dutch cultural expenditure goes to Amsterdam, simply because most of the national art and cultural institutions are located there. While it is true that the whole country makes use of them, the minister felt that this should not mean that the rest must remain a barren plain, certainly not Rotterdam which in terms of number of inhabitants was making great financial efforts to stimulate a lively cultural climate. All the museums in Rotterdam up to then had been municipal institutions. Brinkman's view was supported by a majority in parliament, despite understanding for the opposing arguments voiced by many people and institutions, including at various hearings of the Lower Chamber committees on architecture and culture.

For one of the component parts of the future NAI, the board of Stichting Wonen, exchanging its birthplace for Rotterdam was a hard pill to swallow. The imposition of a diktat did not augur well for the desired independence of the institute. Furthermore, the chances of attracting the public to the somewhat out-of-the-way, sombre ex-library were not considered very high, certainly not in comparison with a location in Amsterdam's Berlage's Beurs. In January 1985 the board of Stichting Wonen began to make difficulties, announcing that it would no longer participate in preparations for the new institute. This was awkward for the minister because the regular subsidy to Stichting Wonen was supposed to form part of the subsidy for the future NAI.

After a year of fruitless talk, a mediator was found in the person of Prof. Piet Sanders, known for his arbitration skills and his love of art. From Stichting Wonen he heard that apart from the possibilities in Amsterdam, only a new building near the Boijmans Van Beuningen Museum would give the institute a reasonable starting position in Rotterdam. With this, Sanders was able to work out the core of an agreement in mid-1986 which opened the way to both the foundation of the NAI and the new building for the NAI. His findings were brief and to the point: once the minister had indicated that the financing of a new building was assured, Stichting Wonen would collaborate on the founding of the institute in Rotterdam; the old library should in any case not be used as accommodation, not even temporarily. The Minister Elco Brinkman, his colleague Ed Nijpels of Housing, Spatial Development and Environment (VROM) and the other cabinet members were able to accept this. Initially, Rotterdam was not happy with the idea of a new building. There were still doubts as to whether the state would be able to find the money for this, raising the possibility of postponement and finally, cancellation. Ultimately, the city council took the risk and building land in the Museumpark was provided free of charge at the suggestion of Alderman Joop Linthorst, the driving force in bringing the NAI to Rotterdam.

Programme and choice of architect
After reaching agreement on the founding and location of the NAI in Rotterdam and on the new building, the initiators were faced with what was for them an unfamiliar task. From the contemplation of architecture and the stimulation of interest in design, they now had to switch to the concrete creation of a building. The exemplary discharge of the role of client is rather different from running archives and forming opinions. A task of a completely different nature was the search for a way in which state involvement and private initiative could be effectively intertwined. In a successful team, both dynamism and control had to be given equal weight.

In the summer of 1986, government ministers Elco Brinkman (WVC) and Ed Nijpels (VROM) appointed a steering group headed by Jan Jessurun. The other members were Mariet Willinge of the NDB, Nic. Tummers of the SAM, Ruud Brouwers of Stichting Wonen, government architect Frans van Gool, Cato Cremer of the Ministry of WVC, later succeeded by Ton Idsinga, and José Loschacoff, adviser to the minister of housing. The steering group in turn appointed various working groups whose members included Bernard Colenbrander of the NDB and Beatrijs Lubbers of Stichting Wonen.

With the acquiescence of the three merger partners – the three institutions which were to merge to form the NAI – Brinkman appointed the organization expert Hans Andersson of AEF in Utrecht as project leader, as well as secretary of the steering group. After the founding of the NAI, Andersson functioned for a while as acting director until the appointment of a permanent director in 1989: Adri Duivesteijn, former alderman of urban development and renewal in The Hague, who had previously served on the board of the NAI at the invitation of the minister of housing. In the very early stages of

the run-up to the NAI, the staff of the merger partners had decided not to appoint a director from among their own ranks in order to strengthen the future institute at the top and to mark the new unity.

In mid-1986 an enormous pile of work awaited the steering group and the various working groups: to formulate statutes and a policy plan, to assemble a board, to set up the NAI as an organization, develop a structure for running it, arrange temporary accommodation for the organization, draw up a social plan for those members of staff of the merging institutions who were going with them to Rotterdam and for the staff who could not or would not go. Equally important and urgent was the task of client for the new building, which involved writing out the building programme and making sound financial preparations.

Naturally, the question arose as to whether a board and a director was needed before the major part of these steps could be taken. However, the steering group considered itself capable of setting energetically to work to prepare the ground for a future board. The steering group's approach was rather pragmatic: there is no question of beginning with a clean slate so let us strike now while the iron is hot and with appointments it is always a question of jumping aboard a moving train.

When an architecture institute makes a new building there is an almost immediate expectation that an exceptional building will be produced. This heavy responsibility did not lead to nervousness, but to a business-like approach to the design task, with support in formulating the building programme being obtained from the Advice Centre of the Government Buildings Department. The writing out of a programme is recognized as a delicate task. The functioning of the desired building must be conjured up as fully as possible, without degenerating into a mere representation of forms and descriptions derived from this. It is not unusual for a client to confine himself to a short formulation of his wishes and then go on to develop the brief with the designer. Some architects regard such a method as creative start to the design process. The steering group, armed with a clear image of the goal and tasks of the NAI, took a different approach. In their view the more precisely the programme is formulated beforehand to give a picture of the use – not of the form – the greater source of inspiration it can be for the architect.

The future use of a building, the ideas that can be formed about it, is most closely related to the policy the client has in mind with regard to the development of his activities. For the architect faced with designing a suitable building, the policy plan and the description of the structure of the organization linked to it, together with the building programme, form a single whole. The NAI's first policy plan, still called a 'sketch' since there was as yet no board to approve it, had as its motto: 'History as a source of inspiration for the contemporary design task'. It signifies the effort to discover everything that is hidden in architecture and to make it known to everyone who wants to hear and see it. The policy sketch indicated three main, closely related, tasks: to compile, manage and make accessible the collections and archives including library and document files, to study all this material as well as keeping abreast of current developments, and finally to communicate the findings to the public in the form of exhibitions, publications and manifestations. Three keywords were attached to these tasks: treasury, study hall and reception hall. The last keyword signalled the intention of enabling the public to enjoy architecture.

The building programme demanded a total of around 8000 m² net floor space, with roughly half going to the storage of collections and archives, which like the service rooms are not accessible to the public. With regard to this last point, the brief contained a description in which the NAI indicated the atmosphere the building must radiate: 'Despite the fact that the

programme aims at a partly closed character the building must nevertheless be attractive and easily accessible to a large public. There is a paradox here, a closed and open character, which can be turned into a stimulus for the design.' One more sentence from the description: 'The building, its immediate surroundings, the interior, the layout, reflect the fact that it is an institution in which the cultural, thematic and practical significance of designing is central.'

Apart from approaching an architect directly, it is also possible to choose an architect by means of a 'multiple commission' or a 'project competition'. Architects who participate in a project competition do so without remuneration and under a motto, so that their names are unknown when the jury announces the winner who is to receive the definitive commission. This procedure allows a client who is not at home in architecture to find a designer who is competent but completely unknown to him, unless of course the jury is of the opinion that the entries are below par and no winner can be designated. The multiple commission is a form of invited competition in which the participants, who are paid a fee for their work, are known in advance and the client plays an active role. He invites several architects with whom he would in principle like to make the project. The procedure entails setting up an assessment committee that evaluates each plan in the light of the brief, but without assigning an order of merit. Since the client himself makes the final choice, he can also ignore the assessment and choose none of the invited architects.

Although it is not a cheap procedure, the NAI decided to hold a multiple commission. It is easier to awaken public interest in architecture and design ideas – one of the NAI's goals – with an exhibition of several plans than with a single design. In taking this decision a consideration of a completely different nature carried much weight. By the time the plans had to be submitted, the board of the NAI would have been formed and could then make a definitive decision. This is indeed what happened. In September 1988 the steering group stepped down leaving behind a substantial report on the results of the multiple commission and some advice to the board.

Minister Brinkman proved ready to subsidize a multiple commission involving six architects and an exhibition of the plans. He also agreed that foreign architects could be invited to participate, but no more than two out of the six. The emphasis had to be on a manifestation of Dutch culture. A long list of candidates was finally reduced to the Dutchmen Benthem Crouwel, Jo Coenen, Rem Koolhaas (OMA) and Wim Quist, plus Luigi Snozzi from Locarno and Ralph Erskine from Stockholm. The latter had to drop out at the last minute for personal reasons, and another Dutchman, Hubert-Jan Henket, was invited in his place. The NAI preparatory group felt that both younger and older architects had to be represented. And apart from a natural weighing up at the individual level, there was a deliberate attempt to represent different movements or tendencies, with current validity as the criterion for inclusion. The architects invited did indeed stand for various orientations, ranging from technical functionalism to eclectic monumentalism. Strikingly enough there was no representative of the so-called Forum group in the Netherlands (called after the journal Forum), also known as structuralism, while its opposite, rationalism (Carel Weeber and his followers) turned out to be equally un-represented. The multiple commission formally began on 15 January 1988 and the designs had to be delivered on 1 June of that year.

In a former warehouse on the IJ in Amsterdam, after the plans had been viewed by the architectural press – resulting in a flood of publications – the assessment committee went about its work in seclusion. This included, among other things, the designers coming to give a commentary. The commission was as follows: architect Jan Dirk Peereboom Voller (chairman), architect Alexander Bodon, professor of construction science Dick Dicke, and Ronald de Leeuw, the then director of the Van Gogh Museum. Planner Hans van der Cammen of the University of Amsterdam acted as secretary. The steering group and later also the board of the NAI regarded the report of the assessment committee as a private recommendation to the client that should not be published. However, from various statements by committee members it could be deduced that they had found the plans to be of a very high standard and that considering the function of the NAI, a powerful visual expression would weigh heavily in the final assessment. It also leaked out that the designs by Jo Coenen and Rem Koolhaas/OMA had received the most positive recommendations.

In the meantime, the board of the NAI had been formed, with as chairman Pieter Beeleaerts van Blokland, governor of the province of Utrecht and a former minister of housing among other things. The other members were Fons Asselbergs, Hoos Blotkamp, Ig Caminada, Adri Duivesteijn, Benno Premsela, Fons Verheijen and Yap Hong Seng. As observer from the Ministry of WVC Ton Idsinga was part of this company. The report of the assessing committee and the recommendations of the former steering group were not the only documents to land on the client's table. There were also numerous other documents, from Aronsohn consultant engineers as costs experts, the Advice Centre of the Government Buildings Service, the Rotterdam Department of Urban Development and from the staff of the NAI. On top of this, there were many articles from newspapers and journals from which the design by Rem Koolhaas generally emerged as favourite. The contents of all these documents and a study of the designs prompted the board to decide to ask three of the architects – Rem Koolhaas, Wim Quist and Jo Coenen – for further commentary. On 3 October 1988 the NAI issued a press release to the effect that it had been decided to commission Jo Coenen to make the definitive design. A quote from the board's statement: 'Coenen's design gives an emphatically expressive and differentiated visualization of the institute functions. In the design of the building parts he does not strive to achieve a pronounced modernism, but rather a timeless repertoire with which the equivalence of the historical and the contemporary as stated in the institute's formulation are visualized.' The practicability, the expression and the references to the history of architecture in Jo Coenen's design, the last linking up with a motif in the NAI's policy plan, were decisive factors for choosing it above the conceptual power acknowledged to be present in the design by Rem Koolhaas and his Office for Metropolitan Architecture. Although lengthy deliberations suggested that it had been a difficult decision, it was taken with a comfortable majority of votes.

Museumpark Rotterdam

By pressing for the new building in the near vicinity of the Boijmans Van Beuningen Museum, the NAI lent impetus to the latent idea of a Museumpark. In 1974, as the first move in a new museum policy, Adriaan van der Staay, then director of the Rotterdam Arts Council (RKS) launched the plan for a *People's park of culture*, based on the park near the Boijmans Van Beuningen Museum in the 'Land of Hoboken', called after its former owner. Van der Staay argued for a concentration of museums in the area. The plan had faded into the background due to a lack of finance.

The municipality had originally reserved a piece of land in the park for the NAI beside the Boijmans Van Beuningen Museum. When the building programme for the NAI's new building revealed that it would be almost twice as big as anticipated, the municipality decided to designate a building site on the other side, on Hobokenplein, an abandoned enclave for parking cars. The area is within the so-called Park Triangle, one of the three theme areas

(along with Centrumruit and Waterstad) of the Inner-city Plan for Rotterdam 1985-1990 which was published as 'the scenario for the last round of reconstruction.' The theme of the park triangle is 'culture and recreation'.

In the context of the Inner-city Plan, the Department of Urban Development, now part of the newly formed Department of Town Planning and Public Housing, headed by director Riek Bakker, threw itself into the redesign of what from that moment on was officially called Museumpark. A broad, straight promenade, laid longitudinally along the north-south axis of the park and designated as 'development axis' and 'connection', formed the main motif in the preliminary study for Museumpark and was also handed to the NAI as guideline for the development of the new building.

In issuing the multiple commission, the NAI insisted on the freedom to not impose the axis at the level of the building site as a diktat on the architects, or in the language of the municipal department, 'a strictly straight extension is not desired unconditionally.' The then government architect Frans van Gool, acting as consultant to the NAI, encouraged the steering group to secure this leeway. Of the given building site, somewhat more than half had to remain unbuilt, including the extremely unfortunate trajectory of a large sewage pipe, a so-called collector sewer. Considering the situation, it was also a condition that the new building must have a 'facade character' on all sides. Still more restrictions would have produced a straitjacket, which runs counter to the objective of a multiple commission to elicit unexpected results. In retrospect, this resistance created the space for awarding the definitive commission to Jo Coenen.

When a private individual or institution wants to realize a building at a strategic spot in the city with an original architect, conflict with the municipality can easily arise. Who is actually making the city? Even if the town planning regulations are faithfully adhered to, one architect will come up with a more suitable response than another one for the same building. It was therefore to be expected that the director of the Department of Urban Development would deliver a judgment on the results of the NAI's multiple commission. At the beginning of July 1988 the board of the NAI received the report of an extensive, systematic assessment of the designs submitted, in terms of town planning and technical limiting conditions and of architectural appearance.

Riek Bakker's conclusion was to the effect that Rem Koolhaas's plan emerged as best in all respects. The board was earnestly requested to take this assessment into account when choosing the winning architect. An 'impact and effect' was discerned in the plans of Coenen and Snozzi, which fitted into the urban structure and the ambitions of the municipality, but with the proposed ponds and bridges and the required shifting of the by now infamous collector sewer, they entailed too many technical and financial complications. The assessment reflected Riek Bakker's predilection for the development axis projected in the park. Koolhaas fitted in perfectly with this, the other designers did not; Coenen and Snozzi even radically rejected the dead straight promenade.

The municipality of Rotterdam magnanimously accepted the decision of the NAI board to designate Jo Coenen as architect. Full cooperation was given in the creation of the NAI pond, although it was not possible to link it to the water in the park and the collector sewer had to stay where it was, so that it determined the level of the NAI complex. In order to have the water level above the pipes, Coenen had to raise his building. Nor could the transformation of the section of Mathenesserlaan between Rochussenstraat and Westersingel into a component of the Museumpark go ahead. Coenen proposed giving the avenue portals and converting it into a broad gravel path with lime trees and seats. For understandable reasons, the fragmentation of a through-road, one of her cherished 'long lines' in the city, was too much for the director of Urban Development to swallow.

After the NAI board had chosen Jo Coenen, the municipality commissioned Rem Koolhaas to design the Kunsthal and to make a definitive plan for the park. OMA's Kunsthal, which is now in place on the southern side of the Museumpark at Westzeedijk, has been acclaimed by architectural critics. The Museumpark has also been laid out, not as the department had imagined, but still less in line with Jo Coenen's suggestions for a traditional park with clumps of trees and broad green meadows.

Together with the French landscape architect Yves Brunier, who died in 1991, Rem Koolhaas made an emphatically artificial urban park, not a representation of nature but a joyful picture of disciplined vegetation and sweet cliches of the so-called unspoiled. There was consultation between Koolhaas and Coenen about the park design, with numerous sketches faxed back and forth, but there was no logical link up to the NAI ensemble. Although the park is not big, it was divided longitudinally into four markedly different zones through which a path runs, the residue of the previously propagated axis. One of these zones is the partly paved site of the Kunsthal, on which Villa Dijkzigt also stands, the former home of Mr Van Hoboken which now houses the Natuurmuseum (Museum of Natural History) which was renovated and extended by Erick van Egeraat in 1995. Then there is a romantic zone with a sparkling mountain brook bed, clumps of tress, exuberant flowerbeds, wandering paths, seats and a panoramic path which has been raised to form a bridge. There then follows an event space with airport lighting, an asphalt surface divided up into compartments, provided with a pattern of connections to pipes and drains. Finally, in a pale carpet of shells opposite the NAI reflected in its pool, there is a tightly geometrically planted apple orchard.

Preliminary design NAI, 1988,
division of the building
volume. Black fineliner and
coloured pencil on drawing
paper, 29.5 x 47 cm

Preliminary design NAI, 1988,
high building opposite the
tower of the Boijmans Van
Beuningen Museum. Black
fineliner and coloured pencil
on drawing paper, 37 x 41 cm

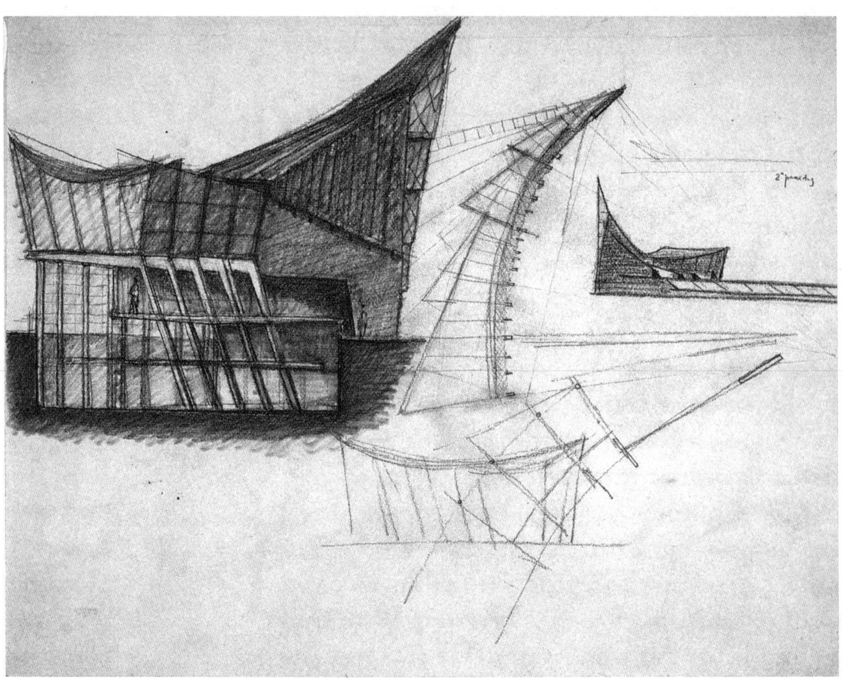

Preliminary design NAI,
Easter Monday 1988. Charcoal
and brown chalk on paper,
40 x 50 cm

Finances and builders

In the catalogue accompanying the exhibition *Six designs for the Dutch Architecture Institute*, which was held by the NAI in the Boijmans Van Beuningen Museum from 9 July to 28 August 1988, it was written hopefully: 'The time scheme of the designing, building and furnishing of the building indicates that the building will be open to the public at the beginning of 1992 at the latest.' In fact, at the moment when the opening should have been taking place, construction was just starting, and even this start hung by a thread. The delay had everything to do with money, but to leave it at this simple explanation would be to give the wrong impression.

Before a thorough building programme had been drawn up, from which a realistic estimate of the costs could be derived, the government had fixed the budget irrevocably at 22.5 million guilders and not a cent more, with 10 million coming from the Ministry of Health, Welfare and Culture and 12.5 million from the Ministry of Housing, Spatial Development and Environment, which would not be involved in the running of the NAI. A prognosis by the Advice Centre of the Government Buildings Department revealed that the programme could be realized for this sum, if minimum prices were adhered to in realizing various parts of the Coenen plan. From the very beginning, the client, having opted for Coenen, clearly not the cheapest solution, was in an awkward situation. On the one hand there was the responsibility to create an optimal accommodation with, bearing in mind the nature of the NAI, some architectural glamour. On the other hand, the budget imposed extreme soberness. For years, the gulf between ambitions and budget stared hollow-eyed at all parties involved in the new building.

Any building intended for art and culture is subject to careful scrutiny. One person looks at it full of expectation, believing that in a matter of culture frugality is an abomination. The other considers the usefulness of art to be merely relative in the light of all the other needs of society and wants the government to keep a tight hold on the purse strings. In addition, the wounds inflicted in the 1980s by the enormous cost overruns associated with the building of the Muziektheater in Amsterdam (the Stopera, a combination of city hall and opera house by the architects Cees Dam and Wilhelm Holzbauer) were still fresh. Against this background, the board of the NAI and director Adri Duivesteijn, who within the NAI had taken charge of preparations for the building, were justifiably wary about starting work on the building before there was a prospect of a satisfactory building and adequate financial cover.

The problem of the budget had already arisen in the awarding of the multiple commission. On the basis of the available 22.5 million guilders, the cost of the construction work, including services and site facilities, was calculated at 14 million guilders by the steering group. Other elements of a total building investment include the interest costs, preparation and guidance costs, and the sum involved in fitting-out. VAT is a separate chapter. The invited architects immediately questioned whether the building programme was not asking too much for such a sum. Because the compulsorily imposed sum did not allow for any frivolity, Wim Quist later felt unfairly rebuffed by the judgment that his design showed little expressiveness, especially when it gradually became clear that the board of the NAI and the chosen architect were wriggling out of the straitjacket imposed by the steering group. On closer examination, Jo Coenen was unable, in mid-1989, to come up with a sum lower than 16.5 million guilders for the construction work. The board followed him in this and in doing so shifted the course laid down by the steering group.

Long before the contractor Strukton Bouwprojekten bv started work in January 1992, an attempt was made to reach a tender, on the basis of the calculations made by Jo Coenen and quantity surveyor Kraan. Orientations showed a discouraging gap of about eight million guilders. The idea that contractors would be eager for the publicity involved with building the NAI proved mistaken; they were more intent on not getting their fingers burned on a building which would be looked at critically. Furthermore, it was a period of great activity on the Dutch building market, so that any economies in Jo Coenen's design were immediately neutralized by price increases.

At a crucial moment in March 1990, when preparations for the building were in danger of becoming bogged down, the Ministry of WVC came up with a million and a half guilders, a contribution to the completely unforeseen costs entailed by the building site in the Museumpark. The Ministry of Economic Affairs provided a subsidy for the exterior walls of the entrance hall and the foyer. These walls, built in structural loadbearing double glazing across two or three floors, developed by Mick Eekhout of Octatube, were viewed as a demonstration project in materials technology. It was then possible, with the help of the Province of South Holland, to secure a subsidy from a European Community fund for improving the economic infrastructure of cities and regions that have fallen behind in this area. The city of Rotterdam, which had already contributed the land, turned out to be prepared to bear another part of the costs, for the layout of the surroundings.

The NAI was able to get its hands on the interest earned by the government money already received for the new building. Furthermore, some progress began to be made in obtaining offers of building materials and furnishing elements at high discounts, a form of product sponsoring. Gradually, a glimmer of light began to appear at the end of the tunnel again.

In the meantime the NAI developed numerous public activities, issued publications and held exhibitions in the temporary accommodation

on the Westersingel in Rotterdam. The postponement of the start of building meant a period in which experiences could be gained which in turn prompted adjustments to the original building programme and thus in Jo Coenen's design. A study centre for research in relation to the collections and archives was added. The exhibition space was also modified to bring it into line with the NAI's productions: more freely divisible and with bigger workshop and storage areas. With an eye to the cultural appeal of Rotterdam, in the making but not yet established or strong by any means, it was necessary, according to Adri Duivesteijn, to create even more incentives to attract the public to Museumpark than previously envisaged. With regard to the exhibition halls and the auditorium in particular, he evoked the image of a theatre with the NAI as the resident company, which also could serve as a centre of activities for other organizations and institutions.

In May 1991, guided by the consultants Bureau Bouwcoördinatie Nederland (BBN), five contractors were invited to submit a tender and an action plan for the building work. The best prices, those of Strukton and IBC builders, were about 4.5 million guilders above the budget for the building (excluding services), which had by then risen to 18 million guilders. After running through the BBN's questionnaires on prices and consultation on alternative realization possibilities, these two contractors drew up new budgets. Although the price was still almost four million guilders too high, it was decided nevertheless to go on talking to Strukton.

A considerably lower tender meant numerous changes in the design, with which Jo Coenen could not agree. He refused permission to realize a modified plan. Finally, in October 1991, an agreement was reached with a fixed price of 21.5 million guilders for the construction work. Construction then proceeded at an astonishing pace, for in January 1993 it was already possible to move the collections, archives and library from the Droogbak in Amsterdam to the 200-metres-long section of the building on the edge of the Museumpark in Rotterdam. In doing so a major automation and ordering operation in the collection was brought to a temporary conclusion.

In the course of 1989, the NAI and Jo Coenen had negotiated an 'exemplary' commissioning situation, assisted by the former government architect Tjeerd Dijkstra in the role of adviser. Exemplary was taken to mean that the architect would not only act as a designer but would then proceed to supervise construction on behalf of the client. This did not happen. On a number of occasions the client felt obliged to call in cost consultants, not only for the negotiations with potential contractors, but also in its contacts with the architect. The NAI had some disappointing experiences with some of these advisers who were expensive and in some cases as much as 30 percent out in their calculations. Once the client was on the right track with Strukton, the engineering office of Grabowsky and Poort was brought in to prepare the start of construction, provide guidance and supervise the process of construction and to coordinate the fitting-out of the building. The architect accepted this. When the building was finished the engineering bureau complimented Jo Coenen because ultimately, when the relation between volume and usable floor space is borne in mind, the work was carried out at a low cost.

Jo Coenen, architect

Jo Coenen (1949) was born and bred in South Limburg, the hilly, European-oriented southeastern extremity of the Netherlands which is to a large degree surrounded by Germany and Belgium. In 1975 he graduated as a civil engineer from what is nowadays known as Eindhoven University of Technology. From childhood on he had a passion for architecture and a drive to be communicative about it. Since his student years he has been active in education, among other things as professor at

the Technical University of Karlsruhe. Nevertheless, a passion to build is uppermost. In a professional practice now spanning twenty-five years, he has produced a great many designs, some forty or so of which have actually been built. They include works on a modest scale, such as shop and home conversions, but also plans on the scale of a suburb or city district. The latter category includes master plans for the former KNSM island in the Eastern Harbour Area of Amsterdam, for the 1100-metres-long Vaillantlaan in The Hague and for the Sphinx Céramique site (23 hectares) in Maastricht.

Jo Coenen displays an idealistic approach to the meaning of his profession and to what architecture can achieve in society. He is opposed to a social reality characterized by specialization, systems and bureaucracy and to the idea that the medium of architecture could not serve as a remedy against this evil. Against fragmentation, dissolution and indifference he proposes the twin concepts of commitment and coherence. In various interviews Coenen has made statements to this effect: 'Our profession is the arranging of material, but our world is not only materiality. There is an idealistic factor. I think that the task is to make noticeable and tangible our commitment to creation, to everything there is.' Another statement: 'For me form is not only important as form, form also has a meaning, when it is able to function in bringing together matters which were previously separate.'

These statements touch upon a theme within architecture which is as intriguing as it is complex. An architect may desire something, for example to effect a good relationship between people and things, something with which Coenen claims to be constantly busy, but the medium of architecture, the creation of spaces with materials, does not communicate in an obvious manner with the many other fields which go to determine the conditions of personal and social life. Furthermore, building, understood as a production process, entails

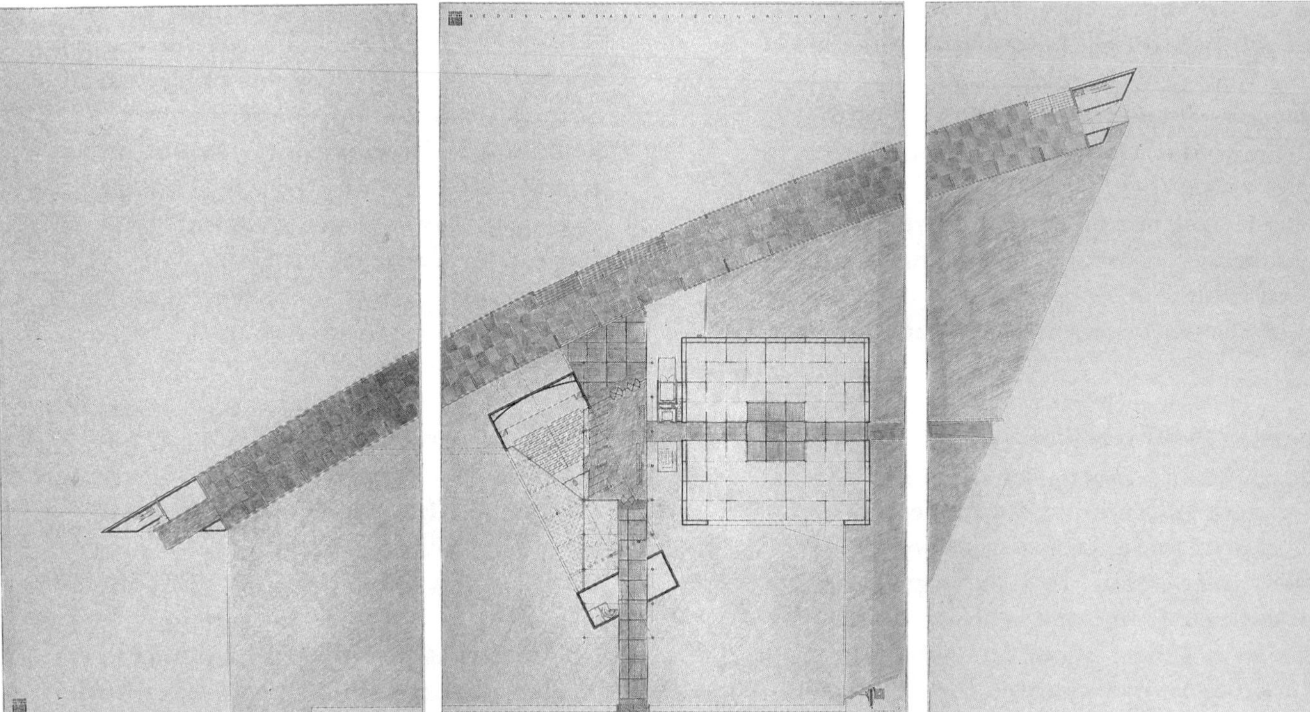

Perspective. Design Jo Coenen, 1988. On the right the tower of the Boijmans Van Beuningen Museum

Triptych with floor plan ground level. Design Jo Coenen, 1988

Maquette of NAI, seen from the south. Jo Coenen design in the context of the multiple commission in 1988

many practical limitations which hinder the expression of clear messages, such as financial preconditions and functional requirements. In addition, the unpredictable retrospective attribution of meanings to buildings that have existed for some time, can turn original intentions upside down.

Intentionally or unintentionally, architecture always reflects a stance. Aimlessness and lack of interest are mercilessly exposed, as is lack of inspiration and superficiality. For significant architecture a pronounced idea is indispensable, but even so questions arise: where does the designer overestimate architecture's guiding effect in society and when do over-literal formal illustrations do violence to architecture? Simplistic slogans are transparent and soon grow threadbare. Herman Hertzberger for example, another architect who is not averse to social pronouncements, takes, notwithstanding his enthusiasm, a cautious attitude in this regard: 'As an architect you cannot do much, so therefore you should not hesitate to do the little that can actually be done. If you think that you cannot improve the world with your work, ensure at the least that it does not become worse.'

Seen against this background, Coenen's statements and his works have an ambiguity, or more carefully expressed, a two-sidedness. The pre-conceived goal of using form as a means of bringing together what he sees as having been wrongly separated, is in contrast to the desire visible in his work to give a building a sovereign or autonomous form. This desire is expressed in the ensemble of the NAI in the autonomous positioning, including rotation of directions and unequal floor heights, of the various parts of the building. After they have been made autonomous, they are then joined together by the organization of the routes which run through the ensemble. As is the case with other works by Coenen, the design of the NAI building reveals a process of creating an individual context, followed by the positioning

of autonomous forms and finally the joining of the various parts into a coherent whole.

Coenen has expressed his devotion to castles, farmhouses, monumental buildings and strong skeletons. By this last he meant the framework-like loadbearing constructions of some factory halls, but especially the mining buildings of his native region. They are examples of autonomous sculptural forms which have an atmospheric effect on the surroundings. It illustrates his urge to allow a building or even parts of buildings to be unique, not dissolved in a structure or fabric. The healing of a fragmented world is therefore not so much a matter of sticking things back together, as rearranging a mosaic. Inspired by the artistic and conceptual aspects in the work of Le Corbusier, Coenen uses the concept of 'definition' for this. Only if a building is given this definition, has a clear individual expression, can it be a part of a valuable environment. As far as he is concerned this also applies to the parts of a building vis-à-vis the entire building and to an urban design plan vis-à-vis its elaboration. Form implies a statement, so one must be as clear as possible in order to avoid haziness and triviality. Only then is communication possible.

The client may regard a strong autonomous form as very important, for he is after all not interested in building something lightweight but rather a building that stands as an eloquent statement. Clients who specifically do no want this, will not be considered here. So in choosing Jo Coenen as architect of the new building, the board of the NAI was able to declare that his provisional design gave 'a decidedly expressive and differentiated visualization of the institute functions.' That 'a timeless repertoire' was mentioned in a positive sense refers to another expression, apart from the tensions between autonomy and context, between standing alone and bringing together, of the duality in Coenen's ideas and practice. He aims explicitly at a contemporary visual expression, but at the same time refuses to accept a dividing line between

what is understood as modernism and
traditionalism. During his training he had
already understood the work of the 20th-
century moderns as an historical source, which
made him loath to reject other sources. In his
quest for definition, all history is at his service,
not just a part of it.

There is nothing naive about the way in
which Jo Coenen wants to express his idealistic
convictions in architecture. A certain measure of
bravado is part of a strategy. He engineers an
infections atmosphere in order to be able to
create what he has in mind. To put it bluntly: he
wants to make what he has in his head. Personal
charm, penetrating arguments and firm
persistence are also exploited as additional
elements in the strategy. For Coenen they are
part of the professionalism he esteems so highly,
both on the practical level and with regard to
theoretical considerations.

The work of Jo Coenen is sometimes called too
calculated, too 'pushy'. Because he supposedly
wants too much as architect, he gets lost in a
lack of restraint, so that his buildings acquire a
relentless quality. Although he counters this
criticism with the remark that restraint is a
euphemism for dullness, Coenen reveals that he
is worried about forcing his work. In designing
he proceeds from a basic set-up derived from
the town planning situation and the building
programme. With a reservoir of received
architectural images at the back of his mind,
particularly those of Le Corbusier and other
avant-gardistes, but also those of the great
masters of other eras, an elaboration takes
place in which light, structure and texture are
considered in that order. In the case of the NAI,
Coenen was heard to say at the time that he
wanted to make use of this task to achieve
greater spontaneity in his work, more
suppleness and naturalness. The exchange of a
clear main form for 'a constellation of forms' is
the result of this. The abandonment of a clear
basic form, which was prompted by the task, is
off-set by an urban manifestation. Although the
achievement of definition is the guiding

principle, fragmentation and stage-setting
reveal increased complexity.

Forms and narratives
On a little sheet of paper there is a scrawled
sketch by Jo Coenen, made with a fine-point
pen. In the same blue ink as the twirling lines is
written in the bottom right hand corner: 'trein
K'ruhe/Koln 28.4.'88'. The sketch shows the
main structure of the NAI which has hardly
altered since that time. The things you can do
on trains. Compared with earlier sketches there
has been an explosion. To begin with, all those
earlier sketches show a single building. No
simple boxes, it is true, but sculpturally
modelled masses. As if we are dealing with a
piece of candy floss, in one sketch a corner has
been pulled up to a height equal to the lantern
on the tower of the Boijmans Van Beuningen
Museum. Another sketch shows a mechanical
insect on tall legs. The scribble made in the
train shows that the building has been
definitively divided into parts. It has been
pulled on so hard from all sides that it had no
option but to break into pieces. These parts are
then stretched again or in fact, shoved into each
other, placed in a spatial context and stitched
into the surroundings as an ensemble.

The voyage of exploration recorded in the
earliest sketches results in a surprising
unravelling, in which numerous elements from
earlier steps have found their place. The soaring
pergola is a sign opposite the tower of the
Boijmans Van Beuningen Museum. The pillars
of the enveloping framework are also the
bearing columns of the transparent central
section comprising entrance hall, the combined
library, reading room and archive study hall,
and office floors. The search for a special
relation with the Boijmans Van Beuningen
Museum has also been expressed in other
components. The almost closed brick box
for exhibitions responds like an echo to the
neighbour across the road, the 1930s brown-red
brick block containing exhibition halls.
Breaking the NAI building into pieces in a

composition of building components seems to have opened up the way for a courtly greeting to the opposite side. If it originally looked as if the building would seek to compete with its neighbour, in the end a gesture of recognition has been made.

The series of sketches betrays the way in which Coenen sets to work when designing. The building programme is important, but is not turned into a sum of functional requirements. Present in the background is an interpretation of the city where the building must occupy a position. As a result of what he calls the 'special vicissitudes' of the city – the fragmentary construction of the city as a by-product of the earlier harbour construction and the wartime destruction followed by rational reconstruction – Coenen sees in Rotterdam an intense interweaving of modern and traditional fragments. With this visual narrative and a whirligig of inspiring examples from architectural history in mind – up to and including the most recent – he looks for a form that is rich in associations. In the case of the NAI Coenen, with his manner of working, also set himself the task of demonstrating the many meanings of architecture, ranging from a practical object for use to a bearer of traditions and social aspirations.

The breaking and kneading of the forms of the NAI into a compelling and simultaneously usable urban ensemble which tells many stories, involved the demolition of an obstructive barrier. More than half the contents of the building consist of closed, air-conditioned windowless rooms for the storage of the collections and archives, the so-called depots. How do you build a bunker in the city that is the largest part of a building supposed to be inviting? The arcade under the extended and curved building section for the collections and archives, killed three birds with one stone. It links together the different parts of the building. As if within wide open arms, the other parts lie sheltered on and in a pond with sturdy banks. The Museumpark is screened off from

the city. At the same time the arcade forms a long series of windows which offer constantly changing vistas into and out of the park. The enormous pergola reinforces this demarcation which is also a point through which to pass, an enclosure and an entrance.

Under the arcade, the curve makes it impossible to see from one end to the other. The rhythm of the round columns and the play of light and shadow which they produce have an infinite-seeming perspective effect, which seems to slowly fade away. The light sculpture by artist Peter Struycken intensifies this effect into a spectacle. It consists of light alone, which at night causes the concrete columns to reflect a glow of bright colours. Controlled by a computer program, the colours change.

There is no shortage of insistent scenes in the daytime either. A trip around the ensemble produces different tableaus each time. Apart from the forms, the contrast between the glass entrance building with office floors above, the sturdy brick building for exhibitions and the collections building brutally clad with metal plates above the arcade, contribute much to this. The reflections in the large pond on the Museumpark side add even more to this. The slender bridge over the water to the entrance hall, marked by a sturdy concrete portal, is suspended like a catwalk ready to be wheeled away at a moment's notice. That too creates a theatrical effect.

Even though the basic structure of the NAI in that April 1988 sketch was retained, numerous changes were introduced after the multiple commission culminated in Coenen being chosen to make the definitive design. Parking, loading and unloading under the arcade, as well as a room layout for the office floors, and a pneumatic dispatch system between the building section with the depots and the archives hall and library in the entrance building all proved to be unrealistic. More far-reaching were the changes made to the building in the interests of the

First sketch of the main layout
of the NAI, dated 28 April
1988, with the note to the
effect that the sketch was
made on the train between
Karlsruhe and Cologne. Blue
fineliner on squared paper,
21 x 30 cm (folded double)

Study of building part for the
exhibitions. Black fineliner and
coloured pencil on drawing
paper, 43 x 30 cm

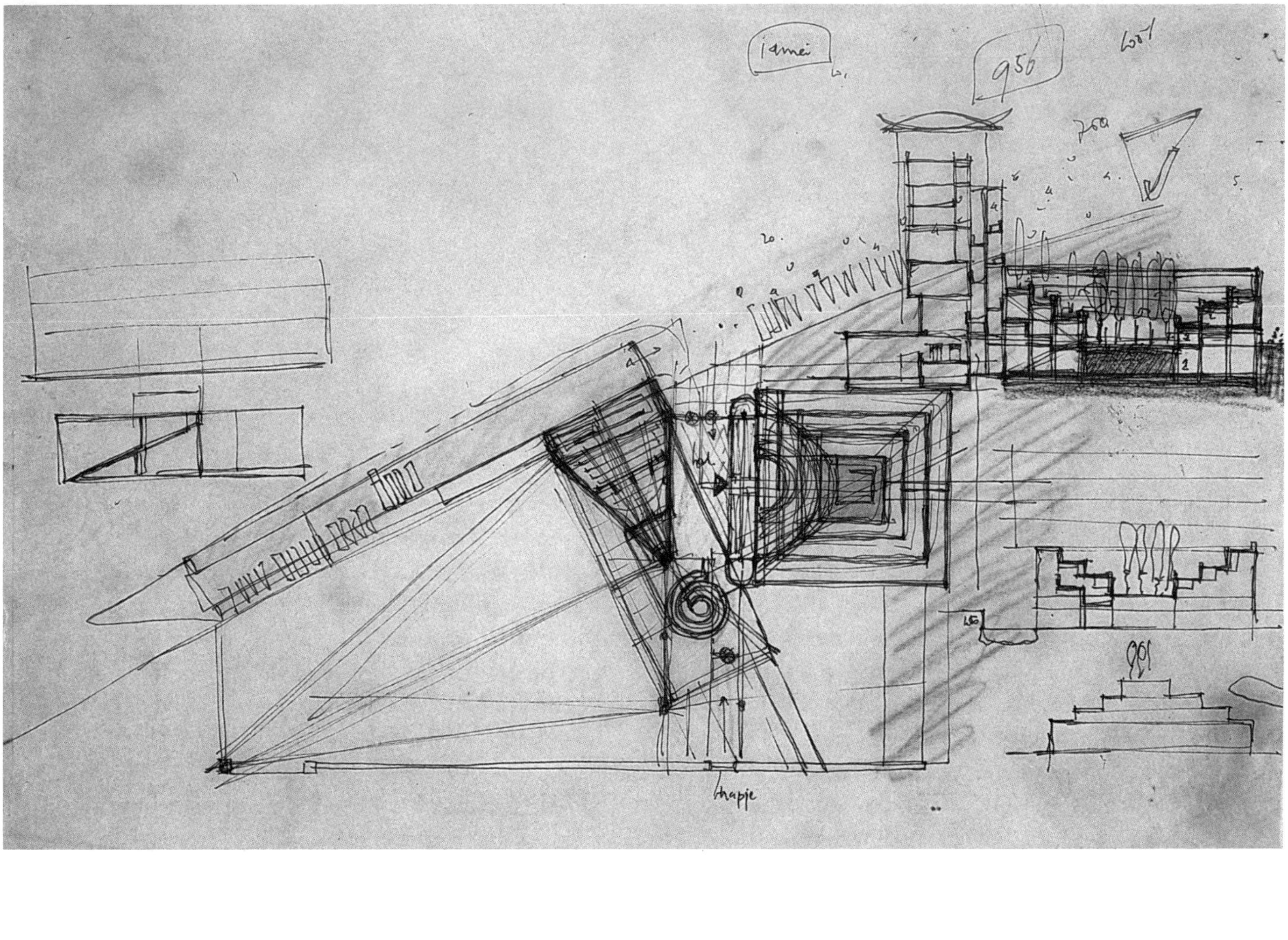

Using a maquette Jo Coenen
explains his design for the NAI,
mid-1989

exhibitions. The hollowing out of the space proposed here and a third entrance route did not chime with the spatial requirements and had to be scrapped. For the workshops and storage areas a more rational elaboration was needed. Space had to be found in the collections building for a study centre. Apart from adjusted requirements on the part of the NAI and the search for more practical solutions, simplifications due to financial considerations also led to changes. In the original design the entrance building consisted of a lower part and a separate superstructure linked by the archives study hall in a free round form. These two parts were combined to form a rectangular box, which meant a considerable saving in building costs. The extremely simple cladding of the walls of the section for the collections and archives must be seen in the light of cost reductions.

The interior also reveals traces of economizing. Nevertheless, here too, as on the exterior, 'the game of stage settings' remains paramount. A wooden platform on steel columns forms the floor of the entire entrance hall, surrounded by Mick Eekhout's glass membrane. A bridge carries the visitors to the circulation core, to the intensely coloured cylindrical ramps or to the lift and stairs going down (foyer with terrace on the water, auditorium and big exhibition hall) or up (other exhibition halls, gallery, combined library, reading room and archive study hall, and offices). Straight ahead, at an angle up or down, this section of telescoped spaces and indentations, offers a torrent of vistas. The refreshment bar and the tables and chairs by the versatile designer Bořek Šípek form a scene in themselves in the foyer. As do Šípek's twisting counters in the entrance hall which mark the bridge to the circulation core. It is sometimes too much the way one section, developed into a definition, overlaps and penetrates the other. Where the big, high exhibition hall, with rows of columns along two walls, a horizontal window along the full width on the pond side and a plinth window opposite, already forms an imposing space, the balcony-exhibition space suspended within it has also been given a dynamic form. On the other hand, the library with reading room and archives study hall creates a more tranquil impression. The high gallery along the double-height walls of books in adapted industrial scaffolding by Magista (also responsible for fitting out the depots in the building section for the collections and archives) is reminiscent of the cast-iron structure of some nineteenth-century libraries. On the top office floor, the director's work-cum-conference room designed by Ben van Berkel and furnished like the other office floors and the reading room and archives study hall with severe USM-Haller furniture, has been turned into a completely autonomous architectural manifestation.

The NAI is part of the Museumpark and marks this park. In the first place the ensemble provides a contrast to the older part of the Boijmans Van Beuningen Museum (1929-1935)

and is at the same time a homage to this building by architect Adrianus van der Steur (1893-1953). There is a striking coincidence with regard to these two buildings. Both Van der Steur, who was often told both approvingly and disparagingly, that he had taken a good look at the Stockholm town hall (1909-1923, architect Ragnar Östberg), and the then museum director Dirk Hannema, wanted an architecture for the new Boijmans Van Beuningen that would rise above the fashion of the time. They sought a universal and timeless architectural expression. When the board of the NAI chose Coenen on the basis of his preliminary design, this choice was explained in part by the argument that in the design of the building sections he had sought not a pronounced modernism, but a timeless repertoire. From this coincidence of desire for the timeless and the way in which the two buildings relate to each other, it can be deduced that the NAI and Boijmans Van Beuningen have a long brotherly future before them.

Ruud Brouwers was one of the moving forces behind the NAI. He also helped to formulate the brief for the building in Rotterdam. Formerly Head of the Exhibitions Department at the NAI, he has been Director of the Netherlands Architecture Fund since May 1997.

Acknowledgements

The construction and furnishing of the Netherlands Architecture Institute was made possible by the Ministry of Welfare, Health and Culture (Architecture Department, Cultural Administration, Office for Employment and Investment Projects and Cultural Administration, Deltaplan Cultural Preservation); the Ministry of Housing, Planning and Environment; the Ministry of Economic Affairs (Senter–PBTS); the Province of South Holland and Renaval Rijndelta (EC Fund); The City of Rotterdam.

The K.P.C. de Bazel Hall has been adopted by the Royal Institute of Dutch Architects (BNA). The BNA and a large number of architectural bureaus affiliated to the BNA contributed to this auditorium, named after the first chairman of the BNA: the architect K.P.C. de Bazel.

The NAI Study Centre has been adopted by the Stichting VSB Fonds.

The library and study hall were adopted by the Bouwfonds Nederlandse Gemeenten; storerooms and archives fittings: Magista and furnishing system, design professor Fritz Haller: USM U. Schärer Söhne GmbH.

For the furnishing of the J.J.P. Oud Hall, furniture designed by J.J.P. Oud was made available by the VSB Bank.

Product sponsorship was received from Akzo Coatings / Sikkens; Bik Bouwprodukten B.V.; CVK Kalkzandsteen; N.V. DLW Benelux S.A. Vloerbedekkingen; Dommelsch Bier, GTI; Ton Haas; Klinkerwerk Hagemeister / Lander Bouw-keramiek; B.V. Verzinkerij Heerhugowaard; Glascentrum Holst; Karbouw, LemsvdVen, Lips Sloten; Reaal Verzekering, BRS Premsela Vonk – designers and architects, Professional Sound Centre; Galerie Steltman; Vitra International; Wuldri Schilderwerken.

The counters in the central hall and the furnishing of the foyer (design Bořek Šípek) were made possible by: Renaval Rijndelta, the Province of South Holland, the City of Rotterdam, the Ministry of Welfare, Health and Culture and the Ministry of Economic Affairs.

The light artwork by Peter Struycken in cooperation with Neomat United Laboratories was made possible by a contribution from the Volker Stevin Development Company bv. The artwork in the pond of the NAI by Auke de Vries could be realized from the proceeds of the special Fund Artwork Museumpark to which many contributed: the City of Rotterdam, private and commercial funds Rotterdam, friends and colleagues of the NAI and the visitors to the preview days. The design fees for the two artists was provided by the Stichting Mondriaanfonds.

Colophon

This publication is a substantially revised edition of the book published in 1993 to coincide with the opening of the new building of the Netherlands Architecture Institute.

Design:
Arlette Brouwers, Amsterdam/Emst
DTP:
Anja Nerrings, Amsterdam
Translation:
Robyn de Jong-Dalziel
Lithography and printing:
drukkerij Mart.Spruijt, Amsterdam
Production:
Marianne Lahr, Astrid Vorstermans, Solange de Boer
Publisher:
Simon Franke

© NAi Publishers, 1998

ISBN 90-5662-088-6

Printed and Bound in the Netherlands

Available in North, South and Central America through D.A.P./Distributed Art Publishers Inc, 155 Sixth Avenue 2nd Floor, New York, NY 10013-1507, Tel. 212 627.1999 Fax 212 627.9484

Illustrations:
Le Corbusier, une encyclopédie, monographie, Parijs 1987, p. 23: p. 60
Anke van Helden: p. 10
H. Kähler, *Kunst van Europa. Het Romeinse rijk*, Amsterdam/Brussel 1965, p. 146: p. 60
Mischa Keijser & Janôt Laval: p. 9
Jannes Linders: cover, p. 11, 21, 23
NAi, collectie Jo Coenen: p. 72, 81
Oswald Mathias Ungers. Architektur 1951-1990 (met bijdrage van F. Neumeyer), Stuttgart 1991, p. 58: p. 59
Heinz Ronner, *Louis I. Kahn. Complete works 1935-1974*, Zürich 1977, p. 329: p. 59
James Stirling, *A.D. Architectural Design Profile*, Great Britain 1982, p. 69: p. 60
Ger van der Vlugt: p. 77, 82